AF397828

William Shakespeare

The Tempest

William Shakespeare

Der Sturm

Übersetzung von August Wilhelm Schlegel

Names of the Actors

ALONSO, King of Naples
SEBASTIAN, his brother

PROSPERO, the right Duke of Milan
ANTONIO, his brother, the usurping Duke of Milan

FERDINAND, son to the King of Naples
GONZALO, an honest old councillor
ADRIAN and FRANCISCO, lords
CALIBAN, a salvage and deformed slave
TRINCULO, a jester
STEPHANO, a drunken butler

Master of a Ship, Boatswain, Mariners

MIRANDA, daughter to Prospero

ARIEL, an airy spirit

IRIS,
CERES,
JUNO,
NYMPHS,
REAPERS, spirits

Other Spirits attending on Prospero

The Scene: A ship at sea, an uninhabited island

William Shakespeare

The Tempest
Der Sturm

zweisprachige Ausgabe
Englisch-Deutsch

*im englischen Original
und in der Übersetzung
von August Wilhelm Schlegel*

aionas

Bibliographische Informationen der Deutschen Nationalbibliothek: Die Deutsche Nationalbibliothek verzeichnet diese Publikation in der Deutschen Nationalbibliographie; detaillierte bibliographische Daten sind im Internet unter http://dnb.dnb.de abrufbar.

aionas Verlag, Marstallstr. 1, Weimar
1. Auflage, 2016
ISBN: 978-3-946571-16-2

Personen

ALONSO, König von Neapel
SEBASTIAN, sein Bruder

PROSPERO, der rechtmäßige Herzog von Mailand
ANTONIO, sein Bruder, der unrechtmäßige Herzog von Mailand

FERDINAND, Sohn des Königs von Neapel
GONZALO, ein ehrlicher alter Rat des Königs
ADRIAN und FRANCISCO, Herren vom Hofe
CALIBAN, ein wilder und missgestalteter Sklave
TRINCULO, ein Spaßmacher
STEPHANO, ein betrunkener Kellner

Ein Schiffspatron, Bootsmann und Matrosen

MIRANDA, Tochter des Prospero

ARIEL, ein Luftgeist

IRIS,
CERES,
JUNO,
NYMPHEN,
SCHNITTER, Geister

Andere dem Prospero dienende Geister

Szene: Ein Schiff auf See, eine unbewohnte Insel

Act I
Scene I

A tempestuous noise of thunder and lightning heard. Enter a Ship-Master and a Boatswain.

MASTER. Boatswain!

BOATSWAIN. Here, master; what cheer?

MASTER. Good; speak to th' mariners. Fall to't, yarely, or we run ourselves aground. Bestir, bestir. *Exit.*

Enter Mariners.

BOATSWAIN. Heigh, my hearts! cheerly, cheerly, my hearts! yare, yare! Take in the topsail. Tend to th' master's whistle. – Blow till thou burst thy wind, if room enough!

Enter Alonso, Sebastian, Antonio, Ferdinando, Gonzalo, and others.

ALONSO. Good boatswain, have care. Where's the master? Play the men.

BOATSWAIN. I pray now keep below.

ANTONIO. Where is the master, bos'n?

BOATSWAIN. Do you not hear him? You mar our labor. Keep your cabins; you do assist the storm.

GONZALO. Nay, good, be patient.

BOATSWAIN. When the sea is. Hence! What cares these roarers for the name of king? To cabin! silence! trouble us not.

GONZALO. Good, yet remember whom thou hast aboard.

BOATSWAIN. None that I more love than myself. You are a councillor; if you can command these elements to silence, and work the peace of the present, we will not hand a rope more. Use your authority. If you cannot, give thanks you have liv'd so long, and make yourself ready in your cabin for the mischance of the hour, if it so hap. – Cheerly, good hearts! – Out of our way, I say. *Exit.*

GONZALO. I have great comfort from this fellow. Methinks he hath no drowning mark upon him, his complexion is perfect gallows. Stand fast, good Fate, to his hanging, make the rope of his destiny our cable, for our own doth little advantage. If he be not born to be hang'd, our case is miserable.

Exeunt. Enter Boatswain.

BOATSWAIN. Down with the topmast! yare! lower, lower! bring her to try with main-course. *(A cry within.)* A plague upon this howling! they are louder than the weather, or our office.

Enter Sebastian, Antonio, and Gonzalo.

Erster Aufzug
Erste Szene

Ein Ungewitter mit Donner und Blitz. Ein Schiffspatron und ein Bootsmann treten auf.

SCHIFFSPATRON. Bootsmann –

BOOTSMANN. Hier, Patron! Was gibt's?

SCHIFFSPATRON. Gut! Sprecht mit den Matrosen! Greift frisch an, oder wir treiben auf den Strand. Rührt euch! rührt euch! *Ab.*

Matrosen kommen.

BOOTSMANN. Heisa, Kinder! Lustig, lustig, Kinder! Frisch daran! Zieht das Bramsegel ein! Passt auf des Patrons Pfeife! – Ei so blase, dass du bersten möchtest, wenn Platz genug da ist!

Alonso, Sebastian, Antonio, Ferdinand, Gonzalo und andre kommen.

ALONSO. Guter Bootsmann, trage Sorge! Wo ist der Patron? Haltet euch brav!

BOOTSMANN. Ich bitte Euch, bleibt unten!

ANTONIO. Wo ist der Patron, Bootsmann?

BOOTSMANN. Hört Ihr ihn nicht? Ihr seid uns im Wege; bleibt in der Kajüte! Ihr steht dem Sturme bei!

GONZALO. Freund, seid doch ruhig!

BOOTSMANN. Wenn's die See ist. Fort! Was fragen die Brausewinde nach dem Namen König? In die Kajüte! Still! Stört uns nicht!

GONZALO. Gut, aber bedenk', wen du am Bord hast!

BOOTSMANN. Niemand, den ich lieber habe als mich selbst. Ihr seid Rat; könnt Ihr diesen Elementen Stillschweigen gebieten und auf der Stelle Frieden stiften, so wollen wir kein Tau mehr anrühren: gebraucht nur Euer Ansehen! Wo nicht, so dankt Gott, dass Ihr so lange gelebt habt, und bereitet Euch in der Kajüte auf Euer Stündlein, wenn es schlagen sollte. – Lustig, liebe Kinder! – Aus dem Wege, sag' ich! *Ab.*

GONZALO. Der Kerl gereicht mir zu großem Trost; mir deucht, er sieht nicht nach dem Ersaufen aus: er hat ein echtes Galgengesicht. Gutes Schicksal, bestehe drauf, ihn zu hängen! Mach' den Strick seines Verhängnisses zu unserm Ankertau, denn unsres hilft nicht viel. Wenn er nicht zum Hängen geboren ist, so steht es kläglich mit uns.

Alle ab. Der Bootsmann kommt wieder.

BOOTSMANN. Herunter mit der Bramstange! Frisch! Tiefer! Tiefer! Versucht mit dem Schönfahrsegel zu treiben! *Ein Geschrei drinnen.* Hol' der Henker das Heulen! Sie überschreien das Ungewitter und unsre Verrichtungen. –

Sebastian, Antonio und Gonzalo kommen zurück.

Yet again? What do you here? Shall we give o'er and drown? Have you a
mind to sink?

SEBASTIAN. A pox o' your throat, you bawling, blasphemous, inchari-
table dog!

BOATSWAIN. Work you then.

ANTONIO. Hang, cur! hang, you whoreson, insolent noisemaker! We are
less afraid to be drown'd than thou art.

GONZALO. I'll warrant him for drowning, though the ship were no stron-
ger than a nutshell, and as leaky as an unstanch'd wench.

BOATSWAIN. Lay her a-hold, a-hold! Set her two courses off to sea again!
Lay her off.

Enter Mariners wet.

MARINERS. All lost! To prayers, to prayers! All lost!

Exeunt.

BOATSWAIN. What, must our mouths be cold?

GONZALO. The King and Prince at prayers, let's assist them,
For our case is as theirs.

SEBASTIAN. I am out of patience.

ANTONIO. We are merely cheated of our lives by drunkards.
This wide-chopp'd rascal – would thou mightst lie drowning
The washing of ten tides!

GONZALO. He'll be hang'd yet,
Though every drop of water swear against it,
And gape at wid'st to glut him.

A confused noise within:

»Mercy on us!« –
»We split, we split!« – »Farewell, my wife and children!« –
»Farewell, brother!« – »We split, we split, we split!«

Exit Boatswain.

ANTONIO. Let's all sink wi' th' King.

SEBASTIAN. Let's take leave of him.

Exit with Antonio.

GONZALO. Now would I give a thousand furlongs of sea for an acre of
barren ground, long heath, brown furze, any thing. The wills above be
done! but I would fain die a dry death. *Exit.*

Doch wieder da? Was wollt ihr hier? Sollen wir's aufgeben und ersaufen?
Habt ihr Lust, zu sinken?
SEBASTIAN. Die Pest fahr' Euch in den Hals, bellender, gotteslästerlicher,
unchristlicher Hund, der Ihr seid!
BOOTSMANN. Arbeitet Ihr denn!
ANTONIO. An den Galgen, du Hund! Du hundsföttischer, unverschäm-
ter Lärmer, wir fürchten uns weniger zu ersaufen als du.
GONZALO. Ich stehe ihm fürs Ersaufen, wenn das Schiff auch so dünne
wie eine Nussschale wäre und so leck wie eine lockre Dirne.
BOOTSMANN. Legt das Schiff hart an den Wind! Setzt zwei Segel auf!
Wieder in See! Legt ein!

Durchnässte Matrosen kommen.

MATROSEN. Wir sind verloren! Betet! sind verloren!

Treten ab.

BOOTSMANN. Was? Müssen wir ins kalte Bad?
GONZALO. Der Prinz und König beten: tun wir's auch;
Wir sind in gleichem Fall.
SEBASTIAN. Ich bin ganz wütend.
ANTONIO. So prellen Säufer uns um unser Leben.
Der weit gemaulte Schurk'! – Lägst du ersaufend,
Zehn Fluten lang durchweicht!
GONZALO. Er wird doch hängen,
Schwür' jeder Tropfe Wassers auch dawider
Und gähnt', ihn zu verschlingen!

Ein verworrner Lärm im Schiffsraum

»Gott sei uns gnädig! –
Wir scheitern! wir scheitern! – Lebt wohl, Weib und Kinder! –
Leb wohl, Bruder! – Wir scheitern! wir scheitern! wir scheitern!«

Bootsmann ab.

ANTONIO. So lasst uns alle mit dem König sinken!
SEBASTIAN. Lasst uns Abschied von ihm nehmen!

Ab mit Antonio.

GONZALO. Jetzt gäb' ich tausend Hufen See für einen Morgen dürren
Landes: hohe Heide, braune Geniste, was es auch wäre. Der Wille dro-
ben geschehe, aber ich stürbe gern eines trocknen Todes! *Ab.*

Scene II

Enter Prospero and Miranda.

MIRANDA. If by your art, my dearest father, you have
  Put the wild waters in this roar, allay them.
  The sky it seems would pour down stinking pitch,
  But that the sea, mounting to th' welkin's cheek,
  Dashes the fire out. O! I have suffered
  With those that I saw suffer. A brave vessel
  (Who had, no doubt, some noble creature in her)
  Dash'd all to pieces! O, the cry did knock
  Against my very heart. Poor souls, they perish'd.
  Had I been any God of power, I would
  Have sunk the sea within the earth or ere
  It should the good ship so have swallow'd, and
  The fraughting souls within her.
PROSPERO.Be collected,
  No more amazement. Tell your piteous heart
  There's no harm done.
MIRANDA.O woe the day!
PROSPERO. No harm:
  I have done nothing, but in care of thee
  (Of thee my dear one, thee my daughter), who
  Art ignorant of what thou art, nought knowing
  Of whence I am, nor that I am more better
  Than Prospero, master of a full poor cell,
  And thy no greater father.
MIRANDA. More to know
  Did never meddle with my thoughts.
PROSPERO. 'Tis time
  I should inform thee farther. Lend thy hand,
  And pluck my magic garment from me. So,

Lays down his mantle.

  Lie there, my art. Wipe thou thine eyes, have comfort.
  The direful spectacle of the wrack, which touch'd
  The very virtue of compassion in thee,
  I have with such provision in mine art
  So safely ordered that there is no soul –
  No, not so much perdition as an hair
  Betid to any creature in the vessel
  Which thou heardst cry, which thou saw'st sink. Sit down,
  For thou must now know farther.

Zweite Szene

Prospero und Miranda treten auf.

MIRANDA. Wenn Eure Kunst, mein liebster Vater, so
    Die wilden Wasser toben hieß, so stillt sie!
    Der Himmel, scheint es, würde Schwefel regnen,
    Wenn nicht die See, zur Stirn der Feste steigend,
    Das Feuer löschte. Oh, ich litt mit ihnen,
    Die ich so leiden sah: ein wackres Schiff,
    Das sicher herrliche Geschöpfe trug,
    In Stücke ganz zerschmettert! Oh, der Schrei
    Ging mir ans Herz! Die Armen, sie versanken!
    Wär' ich ein Gott der Macht gewesen, lieber
    Hätt' ich die See versenket in den Grund,
    Eh' sie das gute Schiff verschlingen dürfen
    Samt allen Seelen drinnen.
PROSPERO. Fasse dich!
    Nichts mehr von Schreck! Sag deinem weichen Herzen:
    Kein Leid geschah.
MIRANDA. O Tag des Wehs!
PROSPERO. Kein Leid.
    Ich tat nichts als aus Sorge nur für dich,
    Für dich, mein Teuerstes, dich, meine Tochter,
    Die unbekannt ist mit sich selbst, nicht wissend,
    Woher ich bin, und dass ich viel was Höhers
    Als Prospero, Herr einer armen Zelle,
    Und dein nicht größrer Vater.
MIRANDA. Mehr zu wissen,
    Geriet mir niemals in den Sinn.
PROSPERO. 's ist Zeit,
    Dir mehr zu offenbaren. Leih' die Hand
    Und nimm den Zaubermantel von mir!

Er legt den Mantel nieder.

    So! Da lieg' nun, meine Kunst! Du, trockne dir
    Die Augen; sei getrost! Das grause Schauspiel
    Des Schiffbruchs, so des Mitleids ganze Kraft
    In dir erregt, hab' ich mit solcher Vorsicht
    Durch meine Kunst so sicher angeordnet,
    Dass keine Seele – nein, kein Haar gekrümmt
    Ist irgendeiner Kreatur im Schiff,
    Die schrein du hörtest, die du sinken sahst.
    Setz' dich! Du musst nun mehr erfahren.

MIRANDA. You have often
    Begun to tell me what I am, but stopp'd
    And left me to a bootless inquisition,
    Concluding, »Stay: not yet.«
PROSPERO. The hour's now come,
    The very minute bids thee ope thine ear.
    Obey, and be attentive. Canst thou remember
    A time before we came unto this cell?
    I do not think thou canst, for then thou wast not
    Out three years old.
MIRANDA. Certainly, sir, I can.
PROSPERO. By what? by any other house, or person?
    Of any thing the image, tell me, that
    Hath kept with thy remembrance.
MIRANDA. 'Tis far off;
    And rather like a dream than an assurance
    That my remembrance warrants. Had I not
    Four, or five, women once that tended me?
PROSPERO. Thou hadst; and more, Miranda. But how is it
    That this lives in thy mind? What seest thou else
    In the dark backward and abysm of time?
    If thou rememb'rest aught ere thou cam'st here,
    How thou cam'st here thou mayst.
MIRANDA. But that I do not.
PROSPERO. Twelve year since, Miranda, twelve year since,
    Thy father was the Duke of Milan and
    A prince of power.
MIRANDA. Sir, are not you my father?
PROSPERO. Thy mother was a piece of virtue, and
    She said thou wast my daughter; and thy father
    Was Duke of Milan, and his only heir
    And princess no worse issued.
MIRANDA. O the heavens,
    What foul play had we, that we came from thence?
    Or blessed was't we did?
PROSPERO. Both, both, my girl.
    By foul play (as thou say'st) were we heav'd thence,
    But blessedly holp hither.
MIRANDA. O, my heart bleeds
    To think o' th' teen that I have turn'd you to,
    Which is from my remembrance! Please you, farther.
PROSPERO. My brother and thy uncle, call'd Antonio –
    I pray thee mark me – that a brother should
    Be so perfidious! – he whom next thyself
    Of all the world I lov'd, and to him put

MIRANDA. Öfter
    Begannt Ihr mir zu sagen, wer ich bin.
    Doch bracht Ihr ab, ließt mich vergebnem Forschen
    Und schlosset: Wart'! Noch nicht!
PROSPERO. Die Stund' ist da,
    Ja die Minute fordert dein Gehör.
    Gehorch' und merke! Kannst du dich einer Zeit
    Erinnern, eh' zu dieser Zell' wir kamen?
    Kaum glaub' ich, dass du's kannst: denn damals warst du
    Noch nicht drei Jahr alt.
MIRANDA. Allerdings, ich kann's.
PROSPERO. Woran? An andern Häusern, andern Menschen?
    Sag mir das Bild von irgendeinem Ding,
    Das dir im Sinn geblieben.
MIRANDA. 's ist weit weg,
    Und eher wie ein Traum als wie Gewissheit,
    Die mein Gedächtnis aussagt. Hatt' ich nicht
    Vier bis fünf Frauen einst zu meiner Wartung?
PROSPERO. Die hatt'st du – mehr, Miranda: doch wie kommt's,
    Dass dies im Geist dir lebt? Was siehst du sonst
    Im dunkeln Hintergrund und Schoß der Zeit?
    Besinnst du dich auf etwas, eh' du herkamst,
    So kannst du, wie du kamst.
MIRANDA. Das tu' ich aber nicht.
PROSPERO. Zwölf Jahr, Miranda, sind es her, zwölf Jahre,
    Da war dein Vater Mailands Herzog, und
    Ein mächt'ger Fürst.
MIRANDA. Seid Ihr denn nicht mein Vater?
PROSPERO. Ein Tugendbild war deine Mutter, und
    Sie gab dich mir als Tochter, und dein Vater
    War Mailands Herzog; seine einz'ge Erbin
    Prinzessin, nichts Geringers.
MIRANDA. Lieber Himmel!
    Welch böser Streich, dass wir von dannen mussten.
    Wie? Oder war's zum Glücke?
PROSPERO. Beides, Liebe:
    Ein böser Streich verdrängt' uns, wie du sagst,
    Doch unser gutes Glück half uns hierher.
MIRANDA. Oh, wie das Herz mir blutet, wenn ich denke,
    Wie viel Beschwer ich damals Euch gemacht,
    Wovon ich nichts mehr weiß! Beliebt's Euch, weiter?
PROSPERO. Mein Bruder und dein Oheim – er hieß Antonio –
    Ich bitte dich, gib Achtung! – dass ein Bruder
    So treulos sein kann! – er, den ich nächst dir
    Vor aller Welt geliebt und ihm die Führung

The manage of my state, as at that time
Through all the signories it was the first,
And Prospero the prime duke, being so reputed
In dignity, and for the liberal arts
Without a parallel; those being all my study,
The government I cast upon my brother,
And to my state grew stranger, being transported
And rapt in secret studies. Thy false uncle –
Dost thou attend me?
MIRANDA. Sir, most heedfully.
PROSPERO. Being once perfected how to grant suits,
How to deny them, who t' advance, and who
To trash for overtopping, new created
The creatures that were mine, I say, or chang'd 'em,
Or else new form'd 'em; having both the key
Of officer and office, set all hearts i' th' state
To what tune pleas'd his ear, that now he was
The ivy which had hid my princely trunk,
And suck'd my verdure out on't. Thou attend'st not!

MIRANDA. O, good sir, I do.
PROSPERO. I pray thee mark me.
I, thus neglecting worldly ends, all dedicated
To closeness and the bettering of my mind
With that which, but by being so retir'd,
O'er-priz'd all popular rate, in my false brother
Awak'd an evil nature, and my trust,
Like a good parent, did beget of him
A falsehood in its contrary, as great
As my trust was, which had indeed no limit,
A confidence sans bound. He being thus lorded,
Not only with what my revenue yielded,
But what my power might else exact – like one
Who having into truth, by telling of it,
Made such a sinner of his memory
To credit his own lie – he did believe
He was indeed the Duke, out o' th' substitution,
And executing th' outward face of royalty
With all prerogative. Hence his ambition growing –
Dost thou hear?
MIRANDA. Your tale, sir, would cure deafness.
PROSPERO. To have no screen between this part he play'd
And him he play'd it for, he needs will be
Absolute Milan – me (poor man) my library
Was dukedom large enough: of temporal royalties

Des Landes anvertraut, das zu der Zeit
Die Krone aller Herzogtümer war,
Wie Prospero der Fürsten; dafür galt er
Der Würde nach und in den freien Künsten
Ganz ohnegleichen. Dieser nur beflissen,
Warf ich das Regiment auf meinen Bruder
Und wurde meinem Lande fremd, verzückt
Und hingerissen in geheimes Forschen.
Dein falscher Oheim – aber merkst du auf?
MIRANDA. Mein Vater, sehr genau.
PROSPERO. Sobald er ausgelernt, wie man Gesuche
Gewährt, wie abschlägt; wen man muss erhöhn,
Und wen als üpp‘gen Schößling fällen: schuf er
Geschöpfe neu, die mir gehörten; tauschte,
Versteh‘ mich, oder formte neu sie. So
Hatt‘ er der Diener und des Dienstes Schlüssel
Und stimmte jedes Herz im Staat zur Weise,
Die seinem Ohr gefiel; war nun das Efeu,
Das meinen herzoglichen Stamm versteckt,
Das Grün mir ausgesogen. – Doch du hörst nicht.
MIRANDA. O lieber Herr, ich tu‘s.
PROSPERO. Ich bitte dich, gib Achtung!
Dass nun ich so mein zeitlich Teil versäumte,
Der Still‘ ergeben, mein Gemüt zu bessern
Bemüht mit dem, was, wär‘s nicht so geheim,
Des Volkes Schätzung überstieg‘, – dies weckte
In meinem falschen Bruder bösen Trieb.
Mein Zutraun, wie ein guter Vater, zeugte
Verrat von ihm, so groß im Gegenteil
Als mein Vertraun, das keine Grenzen hatte;
Ein ungemessner Glaube. Er, nun Herr
Nicht nur von dem, was meine Renten trugen,
Auch allem sonst, was meiner Macht gebührte –
Wie einer, bis zur Wahrheit, durchs Erzählen
Zu solchem Sünder sein Gedächtnis macht,
Dass es der eignen Lüge traut – er glaubte,
Er sei der Herzog selbst, durch seine Stellvertretung
Und freies Walten mit der Hoheit äußerm Schein
Samt jedem Vorrecht; dadurch wuchs sein Ehrgeiz –
Hörst du?
MIRANDA. Herr, die Geschichte könnte Taubheit heilen.
PROSPERO. Um keine Scheid‘wand zwischen dieser Rolle
Und dem zu sehn, für welchen er sie spielte,
Nimmt er sich vor, der unumschränkte Mailand
Durchaus zu sein. Mich armen Mann – mein Büchersaal

He thinks me now incapable; confederates
(So dry he was for sway) wi' th' King of Naples
To give him annual tribute, do him homage,
Subject his coronet to his crown, and bend
The dukedom yet unbow'd (alas, poor Milan!)
To most ignoble stooping.

MIRANDA. O the heavens!
PROSPERO. Mark his condition, and th' event, then tell me
    If this might be a brother.
MIRANDA. I should sin
    To think but nobly of my grandmother.
    Good wombs have borne bad sons.
PROSPERO. Now the condition.
    This King of Naples, being an enemy
    To me inveterate, hearkens my brother's suit,
    Which was, that he in lieu o' th' premises,
    Of homage, and I know not how much tribute,
    Should presently extirpate me and mine
    Out of the dukedom, and confer fair Milan
    With all the honors on my brother; whereon,
    A treacherous army levied, one midnight
    Fated to th' purpose, did Antonio open
    The gates of Milan, and i' th' dead of darkness
    The ministers for th' purpose hurried thence
    Me and thy crying self.

MIRANDA. Alack, for pity!
    I, not rememb'ring how I cried out then,
    Will cry it o'er again. It is a hint
    That wrings mine eyes to't.
PROSPERO. Hear a little further,
    And then I'll bring thee to the present business
    Which now's upon 's; without the which this story
    Were most impertinent.
MIRANDA. Wherefore did they not
    That hour destroy us?
PROSPERO. Well demanded, wench;
    My tale provokes that question. Dear, they durst not,
    So dear the love my people bore me; nor set
    A mark so bloody on the business; but
    With colors fairer painted their foul ends.
    In few, they hurried us aboard a bark,
    Bore us some leagues to sea, where they prepared
    A rotten carcass of a butt, not rigg'd,

War Herzogtums genug –, für weltlich Regiment
Hält er mich ungeschickt; verbündet sich
(So lechzt' er nach Gewalt) mit Napels König,
Tribut zu zahlen, Huldigung zu tun,
Den Fürstenhut der Krone zu verpflichten,
Sein freies Herzogtum – ach, armes Mailand! –
Zu schnödem Dienst zu beugen.
MIRANDA. Guter Himmel!
PROSPERO. Hör', was er sich bedungen, und den Ausgang:
Dann sag mir, ob das wohl ein Bruder war.
MIRANDA. Ich sündigte, wenn ich von Eurer Mutter
Nicht würdig dächte: mancher edle Schoß
Trug schlechte Söhne schon.
PROSPERO. Nun die Bedingung.
Der König Napels, mein geschworner Feind,
Horcht dem Gesuche meines Bruders: nämlich
Er sollte, gegen die versprochnen Punkte
Von Lehnspflicht, und ich weiß nicht wie viel Zins,
Mich und die Meinen gleich vom Herzogtum
Austilgen und zu Lehn das schöne Mailand
Samt allen Würden meinem Bruder geben.
Drauf, als man ein Verräterheer geworben,
In einer Nacht, erkoren zu der Tat,
Schloss nun Antonio Mailands Tore auf,
Und in der mitternächt'gen Stille rissen
Die Diener seines Anschlags uns hinweg,
Mich und dich weinend Kind.
MIRANDA. Ach, welch ein Jammer!
Ich, die vergessen, wie ich damals weinte,
Bewein' es jetzt aufs neu'; es ist ein Wink,
Der Tränen mir erpresst.
PROSPERO. Hör' noch ein wenig,
Dann bring' ich dich auf das Geschäft, das jetzt
Uns vorliegt, ohne welches die Geschichte
Sehr unnütz wär'.
MIRANDA. Warum nicht brachten sie
Zur Stund' uns um?
PROSPERO. Ja, Mädchen, gut gefragt!
Das Vor'ge heischt den Zweifel. Kind, sie wagten's nicht
(So treue Liebe trug das Volk zu mir),
Der Tat solch blutig Siegel aufzudrücken,
Und schminkten schöner den verruchten Zweck.
Sie rissen uns an eines Schifflcins Bord,
Dann ein paar Meilen seewärts; nahmen dort
Ein faul Geripp' von Boot, ganz abgetakelt,

Nor tackle, sail, nor mast, the very rats
Instinctively have quit it. There they hoist us,
To cry to th' sea, that roar'd to us; to sigh
To th' winds, whose pity, sighing back again,
Did us but loving wrong.
MIRANDA. Alack, what trouble
Was I then to you!
PROSPERO. O, a cherubin
Thou wast that did preserve me. Thou didst smile,
Infused with a fortitude from heaven,
When I have deck'd the sea with drops full salt,
Under my burthen groan'd, which rais'd in me
An undergoing stomach, to bear up
Against what should ensue.
MIRANDA. How came we ashore?
PROSPERO. By Providence divine.
Some food we had, and some fresh water, that
A noble Neapolitan, Gonzalo,
Out of his charity, who being then appointed
Master of this design, did give us, with
Rich garments, linens, stuffs, and necessaries,
Which since have steaded much; so of his gentleness,
Knowing I lov'd my books, he furnish'd me
From mine own library with volumes that
I prize above my dukedom.
MIRANDA. Would I might
But ever see that man!
PROSPERO. Now I arise.

Puts on his robe.

Sit still, and hear the last of our sea-sorrow:
Here in this island we arriv'd, and here
Have I, thy schoolmaster, made thee more profit
Than other princess' can, that have more time
For vainer hours, and tutors not so careful.
MIRANDA. Heavens thank you for't! And now I pray you, sir,
For still 'tis beating in my mind, your reason
For raising this sea-storm?
PROSPERO. Know thus far forth:
By accident most strange, bountiful Fortune
(Now my dear lady) hath mine enemies
Brought to this shore; and by my prescience
I find my zenith doth depend upon
A most auspicious star, whose influence
If now I court not, but omit, my fortunes
Will ever after droop. Here cease more questions.

Kein Mast noch Segel; selbst die Ratzen hatten's
Aus Furcht geräumt: da laden sie uns aus,
Zu weinen ins Gebrüll der See, zu seufzen
Den Winden, deren Mitleid, wieder seufzend,
Nur liebend weh uns tat.
MIRANDA. Ach, welche Not
Macht' ich Euch damals!
PROSPERO. Oh, ein Cherubim
Warst du, der mich erhielt! Du lächeltest,
Beseelt mit Unerschrockenheit vom Himmel,
Wann ich, die See mit salzen Tropfen füllend,
Ächzt' unter meiner Last; und das verlieh
Mir widersteh'nde Kraft, um auszuhalten,
Was auch mir widerführ'.
MIRANDA. Wie kamen wir an Land?
PROSPERO. Durch Gottes Lenkung.
Wir hatten etwas Speis' und frisches Wasser,
Das uns ein edler Neapolitaner,
Gonzalo, zum Vollbringer dieses Plans
Ernannt, aus Mitleid gab, nebst reichen Kleidern,
Auch Leinwand, Zeug und allerlei Gerät,
Das viel seitdem genützt: so, aus Leutseligkeit,
Da ihm bekannt, ich liebe meine Bücher,
Gab er mir Bänd' aus meinem Büchersaal,
Mehr wert mir als mein Herzogtum.
MIRANDA. O könnt' ich
Den Mann je sehen!
PROSPERO. Jetzt erheb' ich mich.

Setzt sich auf sein Gewand.

Bleib' still und hör' das Ende unsrer Seenot:
Zu diesem Eiland kamen wir, und hier
Hab' ich, dein Meister, weiter dich gebracht,
Als andre Fürsten können, bei mehr Muße
Zu eitler Lust und minder treuen Lehrern.
MIRANDA. Der Himmel lohn' Euch das! Und nun, ich bitt' Euch
Denn stets noch tobt mir's im Gemüt: Warum
Erregtet Ihr den Sturm?
PROSPERO. So viel noch wisse:
Durch seltne Schickung hat das güt'ge Glück,
Jetzt meine werte Herrin, meine Feinde
An diesen Strand gebracht; mir zeigt die Kunde
Der Zukunft an, es hänge mein Zenit
An einem günst'gen Stern: versäum' ich's jetzt
Und buhl' um dessen Einfluss nicht, so richtet
Mein Glück sich nie mehr auf. – Hier lass dein Fragen.

Thou art inclin'd to sleep; 'tis a good dullness,
And give it way. I know thou canst not choose.

Miranda sleeps.

Come away, servant, come; I am ready now,
Approach, my Ariel. Come.

Enter Ariel.

ARIEL. All hail, great master, grave sir, hail! I come
To answer thy best pleasure; be't to fly,
To swim, to dive into the fire, to ride
On the curl'd clouds. To thy strong bidding, task
Ariel, and all his quality.

PROSPERO. Hast thou, spirit,
Perform'd to point the tempest that I bade thee?
ARIEL. To every article.
I boarded the King's ship; now on the beak,
Now in the waist, the deck, in every cabin,
I flam'd amazement. Sometime I'ld divide,
And burn in many places; on the topmast,
The yards and boresprit, would I flame distinctly,
Then meet and join. Jove's lightning, the precursors
O' th' dreadful thunder-claps, more momentary
And sight-outrunning were not; the fire and cracks
Of sulphurous roaring the most mighty Neptune
Seem to besiege, and make his bold waves tremble,
Yea, his dread trident shake.

PROSPERO. My brave spirit!
Who was so firm, so constant, that this coil
Would not infect his reason?
ARIEL. Not a soul
But felt a fever of the mad, and play'd
Some tricks of desperation. All but mariners
Plung'd in the foaming brine, and quit the vessel;
Then all afire with me, the King's son, Ferdinand,
With hair up-staring (then like reeds, not hair),
Was the first man that leapt; cried, »Hell is empty,
And all the devils are here.«

PROSPERO. Why, that's my spirit!
But was not this nigh shore?
ARIEL. Close by, my master.
PROSPERO. But are they, Ariel, safe?

Dich schläfert: diese Müdigkeit ist gut,
Und gib ihr nach! – Ich weiß, du kannst nicht anders.

Miranda schläft.

Herbei, mein Diener! Komm! Ich bin bereit.
Nah' dich, mein Ariel! Komm!

Ariel kommt.

ARIEL. Heil, großer Meister! Heil dir, weiser Herr!
  Ich komme, deinen Winken zu begegnen.
  Sei's Fliegen, Schwimmen, in das Feuer tauchen,
  Auf krausen Wolken fahren: schalte nur
  Durch dein gewaltig Wort mit Ariel
  Und allen seinen Kräften.
PROSPERO. Hast du, Geist,
  Genau den Sturm vollbracht, den ich dir auftrug?
ARIEL. In jedem Punkt. Ich enterte das Schiff
  Des Königs; jetzt am Schnabel, jetzt im Bauch,
  Auf dem Verdeck, in jeglicher Kajüte
  Flammt' ich Entsetzen; bald zerteilt' ich mich
  Und brannt' an vielen Stellen; auf dem Mast,
  An Stang' und Bugspriet flammt' ich abgesondert,
  Floß dann in eins. Zeus' Blitze, die Verkünder
  Des schreckbar'n Donnerschlags, sind schneller nicht
  Und Blick-entrinnender; das Feu'r, die Stöße
  Von schweflichtem Gekrach, sie stürmten, schien's,
  Auf den gewaltigen Neptun und machten
  Erbeben seine kühnen Wogen, ja
  Den furchtbar'n Dreizack wanken.
PROSPERO. Mein wackrer Geist! –
  Wer war so fest, so standhaft, dem der Aufruhr
  Nicht die Vernunft verwirrte?
ARIEL. Keine Seele,
  Die nicht ein Fieber gleich den Tollen fühlte
  Und Streiche der Verzweiflung übte. Alle,
  Bis auf das Seevolk, sprangen in die schäum'ge Flut
  Und flohn das Schiff, jetzt eine Glut durch mich.
  Der Sohn des Königs, Ferdinand, sein Haar
  Emporgesträubt wie Binsen, nicht wie Haar,
  Sprang vor den andern, schrie: »Die Höll' ist ledig,
  Und alle Teufel hier!«
PROSPERO. Ei, lieber Geist!
  Dies war doch nah beim Strand?
ARIEL. Ganz dicht, mein Meister!
PROSPERO. Sie sind doch unversehrt?

ARIEL. Not a hair perish'd;
    On their sustaining garments not a blemish,
    But fresher than before; and as thou badst me,
    In troops I have dispers'd them 'bout the isle.
    The King's son have I landed by himself,
    Whom I left cooling of the air with sighs,
    In an odd angle of the isle, and sitting,
    His arms in this sad knot.
PROSPERO. Of the King's ship,
    The mariners, say how thou hast dispos'd,
    And all the rest o' th' fleet.
ARIEL. Safely in harbor
    Is the King's ship, in the deep nook, where once
    Thou call'dst me up at midnight to fetch dew
    From the still-vex'd Bermoothes, there she's hid;
    The mariners all under hatches stowed,
    Who, with a charm join'd to their suff'red labor,
    I have left asleep; and for the rest o' th' fleet
    (Which I dispers'd), they all have met again,
    And are upon the Mediterranean float
    Bound sadly home for Naples,
    Supposing that they saw the King's ship wrack'd,
    And his great person perish.
PROSPERO. Ariel, thy charge
    Exactly is perform'd; but there's more work.
    What is the time o' th' day?
ARIEL. Past the mid season.
PROSPERO. At least two glasses. The time 'twixt six and now
    Must by us both be spent most preciously.

ARIEL. Is there more toil? Since thou dost give me pains,
    Let me remember thee what thou hast promis'd,
    Which is not yet perform'd me.
PROSPERO. How now? moody?
    What is't thou canst demand?
ARIEL. My liberty.
PROSPERO. Before the time be out? No more!
ARIEL. I prithee,
    Remember I have done thee worthy service,
    Told thee no lies, made thee no mistakings, serv'd
    Without or grudge or grumblings. Thou did promise
    To bate me a full year.
PROSPERO. Dost thou forget
    From what a torment I did free thee?
ARIEL. No.

ARIEL. Kein Haar gekrümmt,
    Kein Fleck an den sie tragenden Gewändern,
    Die frischer wie zuvor. Wie du mich hießest,
    Zerstreut' ich sie in Rotten auf der Insel.
    Den Sohn des Königs landet' ich für sich
    Und ließ ihn dort, die Luft mit Seufzern kühlend:
    In einem öden Winkel sitzt er, schlingt
    Betrübt die Arme so.
PROSPERO. Was machtest du,
    Sag, mit dem Schiff des Königs, den Matrosen,
    Der Flotte ganzem Rest?
ARIEL. Still liegt im Hafen
    Des Königs Schiff in tiefer Bucht, allwo
    Du einst um Mitternacht mich aufriefst, Tau
    Zu holen von den stürmischen Bermudas;
    Das Seevolk sämtlich in den Raum gepackt,
    Wo ich durch Zauber nebst bestand'ner Müh'
    Sie schlafend ließ; der Rest der Flotte endlich,
    Den ich zerstreut, hat wieder sich vereint
    Und kehrt nun auf der Mittelländ'schen Welle
    Voll Trauer heim nach Napel,
    Der Meinung, dass sie scheitern sahn das Schiff
    Des Königs und sein hohes Haupt versinken.
PROSPERO. Dein Auftrag, Ariel,
    ist genau erfüllt; doch gibt's noch mehr zu tun.
    Was ist's am Tage?
ARIEL. Schon über Mittagszeit.
PROSPERO. Zwei Stundengläser
    Aufs wenigste. Die Zeit von hier bis sechs
    Bedürfen wir zum kostbarsten Gebrauch.
ARIEL. Mehr Arbeit noch? Da du mir Mühe gibst,
    So lass mich dich an dein Versprechen mahnen,
    Das mir noch nicht erfüllt ist.
PROSPERO. Seht mir! Mürrisch?
    Was kannst du denn verlangen?
ARIEL. Meine Freiheit.
PROSPERO. Eh' deine Zeit noch um? Kein Wort!
ARIEL. O bitte!
    Bedenk', ich hab' dir braven Dienst getan;
    Ich log dir nie was vor, versah dir nichts,
    Und murrt' und schmollte niemals. Du versprachst mir
    Ein volles Jahr Erlass.
PROSPERO. Vergisst du denn,
    Von welcher Qual ich dich befreite?
ARIEL. Nein.

PROSPERO. Thou dost; and think'st it much to tread the ooze
    Of the salt deep,
    To run upon the sharp wind of the north,
    To do me business in the veins o' th' earth
    When it is bak'd with frost.
ARIEL. I do not, sir.
PROSPERO. Thou liest, malignant thing! Hast thou forgot
    The foul witch Sycorax, who with age and envy
    Was grown into a hoop? Hast thou forgot her?
ARIEL. No, sir.
PROSPERO. Thou hast. Where was she born? Speak. Tell me.
ARIEL. Sir, in Argier.
PROSPERO. O, was she so? I must
    Once in a month recount what thou hast been,
    Which thou forget'st. This damn'd witch Sycorax,
    For mischiefs manifold, and sorceries terrible
    To enter human hearing, from Argier
    Thou know'st was banish'd; for one thing she did
    They would not take her life. Is not this true?

ARIEL. Ay, sir.
PROSPERO. This blue-ey'd hag was hither brought with child,
    And here was left by th' sailors. Thou, my slave,
    As thou report'st thyself, was then her servant,
    And for thou wast a spirit too delicate
    To act her earthy and abhorr'd commands,
    Refusing her grand hests, she did confine thee,
    By help of her more potent ministers,
    And in her most unmitigable rage,
    Into a cloven pine, within which rift
    Imprison'd, thou didst painfully remain
    A dozen years; within which space she died,
    And left thee there, where thou didst vent thy groans
    As fast as mill-wheels strike. Then was this island
    (Save for the son that she did litter here,
    A freckled whelp, hag-born) not honor'd with
    A human shape.
ARIEL. Yes – Caliban her son.
PROSPERO. Dull thing, I say so; he, that Caliban
    Whom now I keep in service. Thou best know'st
    What torment I did find thee in; thy groans
    Did make wolves howl, and penetrate the breasts
    Of ever-angry bears. It was a torment
    To lay upon the damn'd, which Sycorax
    Could not again undo. It was mine art,

PROSPERO. Ja doch, und achtest groß es, zu betreten
    Der salzen Tiefe Schlamm,
    Zu rennen auf des Nordens scharfem Wind,
    Mein Werk zu schaffen in der Erde Adern,
    Wann sie von Froste starrt.
ARIEL. Fürwahr nicht, Herr.
PROSPERO. Du lügst, boshaftes Ding! Vergaßest du
    Die Hexe Sycorax, die Neid und Alter
    Gekrümmt in einen Reif? Vergaßt du sie?
ARIEL. Nein, Herr.
PROSPERO. Ja, sag' ich. Sprich, wo war sie her?
ARIEL. Aus Algier, Herr.
PROSPERO. Ha, so? Ich muss dir einmal
    In jedem Mond vorhalten, was du bist;
    Denn du vergisst es. Die verruchte Hexe,
    Die Sycorax, ward für unzähl'ge Frevel
    Und Zauberei'n, wovor ein menschlich Ohr
    Erschrecken muss, von Algier, wie du weißt,
    Verbannt; um eines willen, das sie tat,
    Verschonten sie ihr Leben. Ist's nicht wahr?
ARIEL. Ja, Herr.
PROSPERO. Die Unholdin ward schwanger hergebracht.
    Hier ließen sie die Schiffer. Du, mein Sklav'
    (So sagst du selbst aus), warst ihr Diener damals.
    Allein da du, ein allzu zarter Geist,
    Ihr schnödes fleischliches Geheiß zu tun,
    Dich ihrem großen Werk entzogst, verschloss sie
    Mit ihrer stärkern Diener Hilfe dich,
    In ihrer höchsten unbezähmbar'n Wut,
    In einer Fichte Spalt; ein Dutzend Jahre
    Hielt diese Kluft dich peinlich eingeklemmt.
    Sie starb in dieser Zeit und ließ dich da,
    Wo du Gestöhn ausstießest, unablässig,
    Wie Mühlenräder klappern. Damals zierte
    (Bis auf ein scheckig Wechselbalg, den Sohn,
    Den sie hier warf) noch menschliche Gestalt
    Dies Eiland nicht.
ARIEL. Ja, Caliban, ihr Sohn.
PROSPERO. So sag' ich, dummes Ding! Der Caliban,
    Der jetzt mir dienstbar ist. Du weißt am besten,
    In welcher Marter ich dich fand. Dein Ächzen
    Durchdrang der nie gezähmten Bären Brust
    Und machte Wölfe heulen; eine Marter
    War's für Verdammte, welche Sycorax
    Nicht wieder lösen konnte: meine Kunst,

When I arriv'd and heard thee, that made gape
    The pine, and let thee out.
ARIEL. I thank thee, master.
PROSPERO. If thou more murmur'st, I will rend an oak
    And peg thee in his knotty entrails till
    Thou hast howl'd away twelve winters.

ARIEL. Pardon, master,
    I will be correspondent to command
    And do my spriting gently.
PROSPERO. Do so; and after two days
    I will discharge thee.
ARIEL. That's my noble master!
    What shall I do? say what? what shall I do?
PROSPERO. Go make thyself like a nymph o' th' sea; be subject
    To no sight but thine and mine, invisible
    To every eyeball else. Go take this shape
    And hither come in't. Go. Hence with diligence!

Exit Ariel.

    Awake, dear heart, awake! Thou hast slept well,
    Awake!
MIRANDA. The strangeness of your story put
    Heaviness in me.
PROSPERO. Shake it off. Come on,
    We'll visit Caliban my slave, who never
    Yields us kind answer.
MIRANDA. 'Tis a villain, sir,
    I do not love to look on.
PROSPERO. But as 'tis,
    We cannot miss him. He does make our fire,
    Fetch in our wood, and serves in offices
    That profit us. What ho! slave! Caliban!
    Thou earth, thou! speak.
CALIBAN *within.* There's wood enough within.
PROSPERO. Come forth, I say, there's other business for thee.
    Come, thou tortoise, when?

Enter Ariel like a water-nymph.

    Fine apparition! My quaint Ariel,
    Hark in thine ear.
ARIEL. My lord, it shall be done. *Exit.*
PROSPERO. Thou poisonous slave, got by the devil himself
    Upon thy wicked dam, come forth!

Enter Caliban.

Als ich hierher kam und dich hörte, hieß
Die Fichte gähnen und heraus dich lassen.
ARIEL. Ich dank' dir, Meister.
PROSPERO. Wenn du mehr noch murrst,
So will ich einen Eichbaum spalten und
Dich in sein knot'ges Eingeweide keilen,
Bis du zwölf Winter durchgeheult.
ARIEL. Verzeih'!
Ich will mich ja Befehlen fügen, Herr,
Und ferner zierlich spuken.
PROSPERO. Tu' das, und in zwei Tagen
Entlass' ich dich.
ARIEL. Das sprach mein edler Meister.
Was soll ich tun? O sag, was soll ich tun?
PROSPERO. Geh, werde gleich 'ner Nymphe! Dich erkenne
Nur mein und dein Gesicht: sei unsichtbar
Für jedes Auge sonst. Nimm diese Bildung
Und komm darin zurück. Geh! Fort! mit Eile!

Ariel ab.

Erwach', mein Herz! Erwach'! Hast wohl geschlafen:
Erwach'!
MIRANDA. Das Wunderbare der Geschichte
Befing mit Schlaf mich.
PROSPERO. Schüttl' ihn ab! Komm, lass uns
Zu Caliban, dem Sklaven, gehn, der nie
Uns freundlich Antwort gibt.
MIRANDA. Er ist ein Bösewicht,
Den ich nicht ansehn mag.
PROSPERO. Doch, wie's nun steht,
Ist er uns nötig; denn er macht uns Feuer,
Holt unser Holz, verrichtet mancherlei,
Das Nutzen schafft. He, Sklave! Caliban!
Du Erdkloß, sprich!
CALIBAN *drinnen.* 's ist Holz genug im Hause.
PROSPERO. Heraus! sag' ich: es gibt noch andre Arbeit.
Schildkröte, komm! Wann wird's?

Ariel kommt zurück in Gestalt einer Wassernymphe.

Ach, schönes Luftbild! Schmucker Ariel,
Hör' insgeheim!
ARIEL. Mein Fürst, es soll geschehen. *Ab.*
PROSPERO. Du gift'ger Sklav', gezeugt vom Teufel selbst
Mit deiner bösen Mutter! Komm heraus!

Caliban kommt.

CALIBAN. As wicked dew as e'er my mother brush'd
    With raven's feather from unwholesome fen
    Drop on you both! A south-west blow on ye,
    And blister you all o'er!
PROSPERO. For this, be sure, to-night thou shalt have cramps,
    Side-stitches, that shall pen thy breath up; urchins
    Shall, for that vast of night that they may work,
    All exercise on thee; thou shalt be pinch'd
    As thick as honeycomb, each pinch more stinging
    Than bees that made 'em.

CALIBAN. I must eat my dinner.
    This island's mine by Sycorax my mother,
    Which thou tak'st from me. When thou cam'st first,
    Thou strok'st me and made much of me, wouldst give me
    Water with berries in't, and teach me how
    To name the bigger light, and how the less,
    That burn by day and night; and then I lov'd thee
    And show'd thee all the qualities o' th' isle,
    The fresh springs, brine-pits, barren place and fertile.
    Curs'd be I that did so! All the charms
    Of Sycorax, toads, beetles, bats, light on you!
    For I am all the subjects that you have,
    Which first was mine own king; and here you sty me
    In this hard rock, whiles you do keep from me
    The rest o' th' island.
PROSPERO. Thou most lying slave,
    Whom stripes may move, not kindness! I have us'd thee
    Filth as thou art with human care, and lodg'd thee
    In mine own cell, till thou didst seek to violate
    The honor of my child.
CALIBAN. O ho, O ho, would't had been done!
    Thou didst prevent me; I had peopled else
    This isle with Calibans.
MIRANDA. Abhorred slave,
    Which any print of goodness wilt not take,
    Being capable of all ill! I pitied thee,
    Took pains to make thee speak, taught thee each hour
    One thing or other. When thou didst not, savage,
    Know thine own meaning, but wouldst gabble like
    A thing most brutish, I endow'd thy purposes
    With words that made them known. But thy vild race
    (Though thou didst learn) had that in't which good natures
    Could not abide to be with; therefore wast thou

CALIBAN. So böser Tau, als meine Mutter je
    Von faulem Moor mit Rabenfedern strich,
    Fall‘ auf euch zwei! Ein Südwest blas‘ euch an
    Und deck‘ euch ganz mit Schwären!
PROSPERO. Dafür, verlass dich drauf, sollst du zu Nacht
    In Krämpfen liegen, Seitenstiche haben,
    Die dir den Odem hemmen; Igel sollen
    Die Nachtzeit durch, wo sie sich rühren dürfen,
    An dir sich üben; zwicken soll dich‘s dicht
    Wie Honigzellen, jeder Zwick mehr stechen
    Als Bienen, die sie baun.
CALIBAN. Ich muss zu Mittag essen. Dieses Eiland
    Ist mein, von meiner Mutter Sycorax,
    Das du mir wegnimmst. Wie du erstlich kamst,
    Da streicheltest du mich und hielt‘st auf mich,
    Gabst Wasser mir mit Beeren drein und lehrtest
    Das große Licht mich nennen und das kleine,
    Die brennen tags und nachts; da liebt‘ ich dich
    Und wies dir jede Eigenschaft der Insel:
    Salzbrunnen, Quellen, fruchtbar Land und dürres.
    Fluch, dass ich‘s tat, mir! Alle Zauberei
    Der Sycorax, Molch, Schröter, Fledermaus befall‘ Euch!
    Denn ich bin, was Ihr habt an Untertanen,
    Mein eigner König sonst; und stallt mich hier
    In diesen harten Fels, derweil Ihr mir
    Den Rest des Eilands wehrt.
PROSPERO. Du lügnerischer Sklav‘,
    Der Schläge fühlt, nicht Güte! Ich verpflegte,
    Kot wie du bist, dich menschlich; nahm dich auf
    In meiner Zell‘, bis du versucht zu schänden
    Die Ehre meines Kindes.
CALIBAN. Ho, ho! Ich wollt‘, es wär‘ geschehn. Du kamst
    Mir nur zuvor, ich hätte sonst die Insel
    Mit Calibans bevölkert.
MIRANDA. Schnöder Sklav‘,
    In welchem keine Spur des Guten haftet,
    Zu allem Bösen fähig! Ich erbarmte
    Mich deiner, gab mir Müh‘, zum Sprechen dich
    Zu bringen, lehrte jede Stunde dir
    Dies oder jenes. Da du, Wilder, selbst
    Nicht wusstest, was du wolltest, sondern nur
    Höchst viehisch kollertest, versah ich dich
    Mit Worten, deine Meinung kund zu tun.
    Doch deiner niedern Art, obwohl du lerntest,
    Hing etwas an, das edlere Naturen

Deservedly confin'd into this rock,
Who hadst deserv'd more than a prison.

CALIBAN. You taught me language, and my profit on't
Is, I know how to curse. The red-plague rid you
For learning me your language!
PROSPERO. Hag-seed, hence!
Fetch us in fuel, and be quick, thou'rt best,
To answer other business. Shrug'st thou, malice?
If thou neglect'st, or dost unwillingly
What I command, I'll rack thee with old cramps,
Fill all thy bones with aches, make thee roar
That beasts shall tremble at thy din.
CALIBAN. No, pray thee.

Aside.

I must obey. His art is of such pow'r,
It would control my dam's god, Setebos,
And make a vassal of him.
PROSPERO. So, slave, hence!

Exit Caliban. Enter Ferdinand; and Ariel, invisible, playing and singing.

Ariel's Song
ARIEL.
> Come unto these yellow sands,
> And then take hands:
> Curtsied when you have, and kiss'd,
> The wild waves whist:
> Foot it featly here and there,
> And, sweet sprites, the burthen bear.
> Hark, hark!

Burthen, dispersedly, within.

> Bow-wow.
> The watch-dogs bark!

Burthen, dispersedly, within.

> Bow-wow.
> Hark, hark, I hear
> The strain of strutting chanticleer:

Cry within.

> Cock-a-diddle-dow.

Nicht um sich leiden konnten: darum wardst du
Verdienterweis' in diesen Fels gesperrt,
Der du noch mehr verdient als ein Gefängnis.
CALIBAN. Ihr lehrtet Sprache mir, und mein Gewinn
Ist, dass ich weiß zu fluchen. Hol' die Pest Euch
Fürs Lehren Eurer Sprache!
PROSPERO. Fort, Hexenbrut!
Schaff Holz her, und sei hurtig, rat' ich dir,
Um andres noch zu leisten! Zuckst du, Unhold?
Wenn du versäumest oder ungern tust,
Was ich befehle, foltr' ich dich mit Gichtern,
Füll' dein Gebein mit Schmerzen, mach' dich brüllen,
Dass Bestien zittern vor dem Lärm.
CALIBAN. Nein, bitte!

Beiseite.

Ich muss gehorchen; seine Kunst bezwänge
Wohl meiner Mutter Gott, den Setebos,
Und macht' ihn zum Vasallen.
PROSPERO. Fort denn, Sklav'!

Caliban ab. Ariel kommt unsichtbar, spielend und singend. Ferdinand folgt ihm.

Ariels Lied

ARIEL.
    Kommt auf diesen gelben Strand!
      Fügt Hand in Hand!
    Wann ihr euch geküsst, verneigt
      Die See nun schweigt:
    Hier und dort behände springt,
      Und den Chor, ihr Geister, singt!
    Horch! Horch!

Zerstreute Stimmen draußen.

    Wau! Wau!
    Es bellt der Hund:

Zerstreute Stimmen draußen.

    Wau! Wau!
    Horch! Horch!
    Der Hahn tut seine Wache kund,

Ein Schrei draußen.

    Er kräht: Kikiriki!

FERDINAND. Where should this music be? I' th' air, or th' earth?
  It sounds no more; and sure it waits upon
  Some god o' th' island. Sitting on a bank,
  Weeping again the King my father's wrack,
  This music crept by me upon the waters,
  Allaying both their fury and my passion
  With its sweet air; thence I have follow'd it,
  Or it hath drawn me rather. But 'tis gone.
  No, it begins again.

Ariel's Song

ARIEL *sings*.
        Full fadom five thy father lies,
            Of his bones are coral made:
        Those are pearls that were his eyes:
            Nothing of him that doth fade,
        But doth suffer a sea-change
        Into something rich and strange.
        Sea-nymphs hourly ring his knell:

Burthen within.

        Ding-dong.
        Hark now I hear them
        Ding-dong bell.
FERDINAND. The ditty does remember my drown'd father.
  This is no mortal business, nor no sound
  That the earth owes. I hear it now above me.
PROSPERO. The fringed curtains of thine eye advance,
  And say what thou seest yond.
MIRANDA. What, is't a spirit?
  Lord, how it looks about! Believe me, sir,
  It carries a brave form. But 'tis a spirit.
PROSPERO. No, wench, it eats, and sleeps, and hath such senses
  As we have – such. This gallant which thou seest
  Was in the wrack; and but he's something stain'd
  With grief (that's beauty's canker), thou mightst call him
  A goodly person. He hath lost his fellows,
  And strays about to find 'em.
MIRANDA. I might call him
  A thing divine, for nothing natural
  I ever saw so noble.
PROSPERO *aside*. It goes on, I see,
  As my soul prompts it. Spirit, fine spirit, I'll free thee
  Within two days for this.

FERDINAND. Wo ist wohl die Musik? In der Luft? Auf Erden? –
    Sie spielt nicht mehr: – sie dienet einem Gott
    Der Insel sicherlich. Ich saß am Strand
    Und weint' aufs neu' den König, meinen Vater:
    Da schlich sie zu mir über die Gewässer
    Und lindert' ihre Wut und meinen Schmerz
    Mit süßer Melodie; dann folgt' ich ihr,
    Sie zog vielmehr mich nach. Nun ist sie fort;
    Da hebt sie wieder an.

Ariels Lied

ARIEL *singt.*
        Fünf Faden tief liegt Vater dein:
            Sein Gebein wird zu Korallen;
        Perlen sind die Augen sein:
            Nichts an ihm, das soll verfallen,
        Das nicht wandelt Meereshut
        In ein reich und seltnes Gut.
        Nymphen läuten stündlich ihm,
Stimmen draußen.
        Bim! Bim! Bim!
        Da horch! ihr Glöcklein
        Bim! Bim! Bim!
FERDINAND. Das Liedlein spricht von meinem toten Vater.
    Dies ist kein sterblich Tun; der Ton gehört
    Der Erde nicht: jetzt hör' ich droben ihn.
PROSPERO. Zieh' deiner Augen Fransenvorhang auf
    Und sag, was siehst du dort?
MIRANDA. Was ist's? Ein Geist?
    O Himmel, wie's umherschaut! Glaubt mir, Vater,
    's ist herrlich von Gestalt; doch ist's ein Geist.
PROSPERO. Nein, Kind, es isst und trinkt, hat solche Sinne
    Wie wir ganz so. Der Knabe, den du siehst,
    War bei dem Schiffbruch, und entstellt' ihn Gram,
    Der Schönheit Wurm, nicht, nenntest du mit Recht
    Ihn wohl gebildet. Er verlor die Freunde
    Und schweift umher nach ihnen.

MIRANDA. Nennen möcht' ich
    Ein göttlich Ding ihn: nichts Natürliches
    Sah ich so edel je.
PROSPERO *beiseite.* Ich seh', es geht
    Nach Herzenswunsch. Geist! lieber Geist! Dafür
    Wirst in zwei Tagen frei.

FERDINAND. Most sure, the goddess
    On whom these airs attend! Vouchsafe my pray'r
    May know if you remain upon this island,
    And that you will some good instruction give
    How I may bear me here. My prime request,
    Which I do last pronounce, is O you wonder!
    If you be maid, or no?
MIRANDA. No wonder, sir,
    But certainly a maid.
FERDINAND. My language? heavens!
    I am the best of them that speak this speech,
    Were I but where 'tis spoken.
PROSPERO. How? the best?
    What wert thou, if the King of Naples heard thee?
FERDINAND. A single thing, as I am now, that wonders
    To hear thee speak of Naples. He does hear me,
    And that he does I weep. Myself am Naples,
    Who with mine eyes (never since at ebb) beheld
    The King my father wrack'd.
MIRANDA. Alack, for mercy!
FERDINAND. Yes, faith, and all his lords, the Duke of Milan
    And his brave son being twain.
PROSPERO *aside*. The Duke of Milan
    And his more braver daughter could control thee,
    If now 'twere fit to do't. At the first sight
    They have chang'd eyes. Delicate Ariel,
    I'll set thee free for this. – A word, good sir,
    I fear you have done yourself some wrong; a word.

MIRANDA. Why speaks my father so ungently? This
    Is the third man that e'er I saw; the first
    That e'er I sigh'd for. Pity move my father
    To be inclin'd my way!
FERDINAND. O, if a virgin,
    And your affection not gone forth, I'll make you
    The Queen of Naples.
PROSPERO. Soft, sir, one word more.

Aside.

    They are both in either's pow'rs; but this swift business
    I must uneasy make, lest too light winning
    Make the prize light. – One word more: I charge thee
    That thou attend me. Thou dost here usurp
    The name thou ow'st not, and hast put thyself

FERDINAND. Gewiss die Göttin,
    Der die Musik dient. – Gönnet meinem Wunsch
    Zu wissen, ob Ihr wohnt auf dieser Insel;
    Wollt Anleitung mir geben, wie ich hier
    Mich muss betragen; meiner Bitten erste,
    Zuletzt gesagt, ist diese: schönes Wunder,
    Seid Ihr ein Mädchen oder nicht?
MIRANDA. Kein Wunder,
    Doch sicherlich ein Mädchen.
FERDINAND. Meine Sprache! Himmel!
    Ich bin der Höchste derer, die sie reden,
    Wär' ich, wo man sie spricht.
PROSPERO. Der Höchste? Wie?
    Was wärst du, hörte dich der König Napels?
FERDINAND. Ein Wesen, wie ich jetzo bin, erstaunt,
    Dass du von Napel redest. Er vernimmt mich;
    Ich weine, dass er's tut; ich selbst bin Napel
    Und sah mit meinen Augen, ohne Ebbe
    Seitdem, den König, meinen Vater, sinken.
MIRANDA. O welch ein Jammer!
FERDINAND. Ja glaubt es mir, samt allen seinen Edlen,
    Der Herzog Mailands und sein guter Sohn
    Auch unter dieser Zahl.
PROSPERO *beiseite*. Der Herzog Mailands
    Und seine bessre Tochter könnten leicht
    Dich wider legen, wär' es an der Zeit. –
    Beim ersten Anblick tauschten sie die Augen.
    Mein zarter Ariel, für diesen Dienst
    Entlass' ich dich. – Ein Wort, mein Herr! Ich fürchte,
    Ihr habt Euch selbst zu nah getan: ein Wort!
MIRANDA. Was spricht mein Vater nur so rau! Dies ist
    Der dritte Mann, den ich gesehn; der erste,
    Um den ich seufzte. Neig' auf meine Seite
    Den Vater Mitleid doch!
FERDINAND. Oh, wenn ein Mädchen,
    Und Eure Neigung frei noch, mach' ich Euch
    Zur Königin von Napel.
PROSPERO. Sanft, Herr ! Noch ein Wort! –

Beiseite.

    Eins ist des andern ganz: den schnellen Handel
    Muss ich erschweren, dass nicht leichter Sieg
    Den Preis verringre. – Noch ein Wort! Ich sag' dir,
    Begleite mich! Du maßest einen Namen
    Dir an, der dein nicht ist; und hast die Insel

Upon this island as a spy, to win it
From me, the lord on't.
FERDINAND. No, as I am a man.
MIRANDA. There's nothing ill can dwell in such a temple.
If the ill spirit have so fair a house,
Good things will strive to dwell with't.

PROSPERO. Follow me. –
Speak not you for him; he's a traitor. – Come,
I'll manacle thy neck and feet together.
Sea-water shalt thou drink; thy food shall be
The fresh-brook mussels, wither'd roots, and husks
Wherein the acorn cradled. Follow.
FERDINAND. No,
I will resist such entertainment till
Mine enemy has more pow'r.

He draws, and is charmed from moving.

MIRANDA. O dear father,
Make not too rash a trial of him, for
He's gentle, and not fearful.
PROSPERO. What, I say,
My foot my tutor? Put thy sword up, traitor,
Who mak'st a show but dar'st not strike, thy conscience
Is so possess'd with guilt. Come, from thy ward,
For I can here disarm thee with this stick,
And make thy weapon drop.
MIRANDA. Beseech you, father.
PROSPERO. Hence! hang not on my garments.
MIRANDA. Sir, have pity,
I'll be his surety.
PROSPERO. Silence! one word more
Shall make me chide thee, if not hate thee. What,
An advocate for an impostor? Hush!
Thou think'st there is no more such shapes as he,
Having seen but him and Caliban. Foolish wench,
To th' most of men this is a Caliban,
And they to him are angels.

MIRANDA. My affections
Are then most humble; I have no ambition
To see a goodlier man.
PROSPERO *to Ferdinand.* Come on, obey:
Thy nerves are in their infancy again
And have no vigor in them.

Betreten als Spion, mir, ihrem Herrn,
Sie zu entwenden.
FERDINAND. Nein, bei meiner Ehre!
MIRANDA. Nichts Böses kann in solchem Tempel wohnen.
Hat ein so schönes Haus der böse Geist,
So werden gute Wesen neben ihm
Zu wohnen trachten.
PROSPERO. Folge mir! – Du, sprich
Nicht mehr für ihn, 's ist ein Verräter. – Komm,
Ich will dir Hals und Fuß zusammen schließen;
Seewasser soll dein Trank sein, deine Nahrung
Bachmuscheln, welke Wurzeln, Hülsen, die
Der Eichel Wiege sind. Komm, folge!
FERDINAND. Nein!
Ich widerstehe der Begegnung, bis
Mein Feind mich übermannt.

Er zieht und ist begeistert von der Bewegung.

MIRANDA. O lieber Vater,
Versucht ihn nicht zu rasch! Er ist ja sanft
Und nicht gefährlich.
PROSPERO. Seht doch! will das Ei
Die Henne meistern? Weg dein Schwert, Verräter!
Du drohst, doch wagst du keinen Streich, weil Schuld
Dir das Gewissen drückt. Steh nicht zur Wehr!
Ich kann dich hier mit diesem Stab entwaffnen,
Dass dir das Schwert entsinkt.
MIRANDA. Ich bitt' Euch, Vater!
PROSPERO. Fort! Häng' dich nicht an meinen Rock!
MIRANDA. Habt Mitleid!
Ich sage gut für ihn.
PROSPERO. Schweig'! Noch ein Wort,
Und schelten müsst' ich dich, ja hassen. Was?
Wortführerin für den Betrüger? Still!
Du denkst, sonst gäb' es der Gestalten keine,
Weil du nur ihn und Caliban gesehn.
Du töricht Mädchen! Mit den meisten Männern
Verglichen, ist er nur ein Caliban,
Sie Engel gegen ihn.
MIRANDA. So hat in Demut
Mein Herz gewählt; ich hege keinen Ehrgeiz,
Einen schönern Mann zu sehn.
PROSPERO *zu Ferdinand.* Komm mit! Gehorch'!
Denn deine Sehnen sind im Stand der Kindheit
Und haben keine Kraft.

FERDINAND. So they are.
    My spirits, as in a dream, are all bound up.
    My father's loss, the weakness which I feel,
    The wrack of all my friends, nor this man's threats
    To whom I am subdu'd, are but light to me,
    Might I but through my prison once a day
    Behold this maid. All corners else o' th' earth
    Let liberty make use of; space enough
    Have I in such a prison.

PROSPERO *aside*. It works.

To Ferdinand.

    Come on. –

To Ariel.

    Thou hast done well, fine Ariel!

To Ferdinand.

    Follow me.

To Ariel.

    Hark what thou else shalt do me.
MIRANDA. Be of comfort,
    My father's of a better nature, sir,
    Than he appears by speech. This is unwonted
    Which now came from him.
PROSPERO. Thou shalt be as free
    As mountain winds; but then exactly do
    All points of my command.
ARIEL. To th' syllable.
PROSPERO *to Ferdinand*. Come, follow.

To Miranda.

    Speak not for him.

Exeunt.

FERDINAND. Das sind sie auch:
    Die Lebensgeister sind mir wie im Traum
    Gefesselt. Meines Vaters Tod, die Schwäche,
    So ich empfinde, aller meiner Freunde
    Verderben, oder dieses Mannes Drohn,
    In dessen Hand ich bin, erträg' ich leicht,
    Dürft' ich nur einmal tags aus meinem Kerker
    Dies Mädchen sehn! Mag Freiheit alle Winkel
    Der Erde sonst gebrauchen: Raum genug
    Hab' ich in solchem Kerker.
PROSPERO *beiseite*. Es wirkt.

Zu Ferdinand.

    Komm mit! –

Zu Ariel.

    Das hast du gut gemacht, mein Ariel! –

Zu Ferdinand.

    Folgt mir!

Zu Ariel.

    Vernimm, was sonst zu tun ist!
MIRANDA. Seid getrost!
    Mein Vater, Herr, ist besserer Natur,
    Als seine Red' ihn zeigt; was er jetzt tat,
    Ist ungewohnt von ihm.
PROSPERO. Frei sollst du sein.
    Wie Wind' auf Bergen: tu' nur Wort für Wort,
    Was ich dir aufgetragen!
ARIEL. Jede Silbe.
PROSPERO *zu Ferdinand*. Kommt, folgt mir!

Zu Miranda.

    Sprich du nicht für ihn!

Alle ab.

Act II
Scene I

Enter Alonso, Sebastian, Antonio, Gonzalo, Adrian, Francisco, and others.

GONZALO. Beseech you, sir, be merry; you have cause
   (So have we all) of joy; for our escape
   Is much beyond our loss. Our hint of woe
   Is common: every day some sailor's wife,
   The masters of some merchant, and the merchant
   Have just our theme of woe; but for the miracle
   (I mean our preservation), few in millions
   Can speak like us. Then wisely, good sir, weigh
   Our sorrow with our comfort.

ALONSO. Prithee peace.
SEBASTIAN. He receives comfort like cold porridge.
ANTONIO. The visitor will not give him o'er so.
SEBASTIAN. Look, he's winding up the watch of his wit, by and by it will
   strike.
GONZALO. Sir –
SEBASTIAN. One. Tell.
GONZALO. When every grief is entertain'd that's offer'd,
   Comes to th' entertainer –
SEBASTIAN. A dollar.
GONZALO. Dolor comes to him indeed, you have spoken truer than you
   purpos'd.
SEBASTIAN. You have taken it wiselier than I meant you should.
GONZALO. Therefore, my lord –
ANTONIO. Fie, what a spendthrift is he of his tongue!
ALONSO. I prithee spare.
GONZALO. Well, I have done. But yet –
SEBASTIAN. He will be talking.
ANTONIO. Which, of he or Adrian, for a good wager, first begins to crow?

SEBASTIAN. The old cock.
ANTONIO. The cock'rel.
SEBASTIAN. Done. The wager?
ANTONIO. A laughter.
SEBASTIAN. A match!
ADRIAN. Though this island seem to be desert –
SEBASTIAN. Ha, ha, ha!
ANTONIO. So: you're paid!
ADRIAN. Uninhabitable, and almost inaccessible –
SEBASTIAN. Yet –

Zweiter Aufzug
Erste Szene

Alonso, Sebastian, Antonio, Gonzalo, Adrian, Francisco und andre treten auf.

GONZALO. Ich bitt' Euch, Herr, seid fröhlich: Ihr habt Grund
Zur Freude, wie wir alle. Unsre Rettung
Ist mehr als der Verlust; denn unser Fug
Zur Klage ist gemein: an jedem Tage
Hat ein Matrosenweib, der Schiffspatron
Von einem Kaufmann, und der Kaufmann selbst
Zu gleicher Klage Stoff; allein das Wunder,
Ich meine unsre Rettung, aus Millionen
Geschah's nur uns. Drum, lieber Herr, wägt weislich
Leid gegen Trost.
ALONSO. Ich bitte dich, sei still!
SEBASTIAN. Der Trost geht ihm ein wie kalte Suppe.
ANTONIO. Der Krankenbesucher lässt ihn so noch nicht fahren.
SEBASTIAN. Seht, jetzt windet er die Uhr seines Witzes auf; gleich wird
sie schlagen.
GONZALO. Herr –
SEBASTIAN. Eins – zählt doch!
GONZALO. Wenn jeder Gram gepflegt wird, der uns vorkommt,
So wird dafür dem Pfleger –
SEBASTIAN. Die Zehrung.
GONZALO. Ganz recht, denn er zehrt sich ab; Ihr habt richtiger gespro-
chen, als Eure Absicht war.
SEBASTIAN. Und Ihr habt es gescheiter genommen, als ich dachte.
GONZALO. Also, gnädiger Herr –
ANTONIO. Pfui doch! Welch ein Verschwender ist er mit seiner Zunge!
ALONSO. Ich bitte dich, lass.
GONZALO. Gut, ich bin fertig, aber doch –
SEBASTIAN. Muss er reden.
ANTONIO. Was gilt die Wette, ob er oder Adrian zuerst anfangen wird
zu krähen?
SEBASTIAN. Ich sage, der alte Hahn.
ANTONIO. Nein, das Hähnlein.
SEBASTIAN. Gut: was wetten wir?
ANTONIO. Ein Gelächter.
SEBASTIAN. Topp!
ADRIAN. Scheint diese Insel gleich wüst –
SEBASTIAN. Ha ha ha!
ANTONIO. Nun, Ihr habt bezahlt.
ADRIAN. Unbewohnbar und beinah' unzugänglich –
SEBASTIAN. Dennoch –

ADRIAN. Yet –
ANTONIO. He could not miss't.
ADRIAN. It must needs be of subtle, tender, and delicate temperance.

ANTONIO. Temperance was a delicate wench.
SEBASTIAN. Ay, and a subtle, as he most learnedly deliver'd.

ADRIAN. The air breathes upon us here most sweetly.
SEBASTIAN. As if it had lungs, and rotten ones.
ANTONIO. Or, as 'twere perfum'd by a fen.
GONZALO. Here is every thing advantageous to life.
ANTONIO. True, save means to live.
SEBASTIAN. Of that there's none, or little.
GONZALO. How lush and lusty the grass looks! How green!
ANTONIO. The ground indeed is tawny.
SEBASTIAN. With an eye of green in't.
ANTONIO. He misses not much.
SEBASTIAN. No; he doth but mistake the truth totally.
GONZALO. But the rariety of it is – which is indeed almost beyond credit
 –

SEBASTIAN. As many vouch'd rarieties are.
GONZALO. That our garments, being as they were drench'd in the sea,
    hold notwithstanding their freshness and glosses, being rather new dy'd
    than stain'd with salt water.
ANTONIO. If but one of his pockets could speak, would it not say he lies?

SEBASTIAN. Ay, or very falsely pocket up his report.
GONZALO. Methinks our garments are now as fresh as when we put them
    on first in Afric, at the marriage of the King's fair daughter Claribel to
    the King of Tunis.
SEBASTIAN. 'Twas a sweet marriage, and we prosper well in our return.

ADRIAN. Tunis was never grac'd before with such a paragon to their queen.
GONZALO. Not since widow Dido's time.
ANTONIO. Widow? a pox o' that! How came that widow in? Widow
    Dido!

SEBASTIAN. What if he had said »widower Aeneas« too? Good Lord, how
    you take it!
ADRIAN. »Widow Dido,« said you? You make me study of that. She was
    of Carthage, not of Tunis.
GONZALO. This Tunis, sir, was Carthage.
ADRIAN. Carthage?
GONZALO. I assure you, Carthage.
ANTONIO. His word is more than the miraculous harp.

ADRIAN. Dennoch –

ANTONIO. Es konnte nicht fehlen.

ADRIAN. Muss ihr Himmelsstrich von der sanftesten und angenehmsten
Milde sein.

ANTONIO. Milde ist eine angenehme Dirne.

SEBASTIAN. Ja, und sanft obendrein, wie er sehr gelehrt zu vernehmen
gegeben.

ADRIAN. Die Luft haucht uns hier recht lieblich an.

SEBASTIAN. Als hätte sie 'ne Lunge, und zwar 'ne verfaulte.

ANTONIO. Oder als wäre sie aus einem Sumpfe gewürzt.

GONZALO. Hier ist alles zum Leben Dienliche vorhanden.

ANTONIO. Richtig, ausgenommen Lebensmittel.

SEBASTIAN. Die gibt's hier wenig oder gar nicht.

GONZALO. Wie frisch und lustig das Gras aussieht! wie grün!

ANTONIO. Wirklich, der Boden ist fahl.

SEBASTIAN. Mit einer kleinen Schattierung von Grün darin.

ANTONIO. Er trifft nicht weit vom Ziel.

SEBASTIAN. Nein, er verfehlt das Rechte nur ganz und gar.

GONZALO. Aber die Seltenheit dabei ist – was in der Tat beinah' allen
Glauben übersteigt –

SEBASTIAN. Wie manche beteuerte Seltenheiten!

GONZALO. Dass unsre Kleider, so durchweicht in der See wie sie waren,
dennoch ihre Frische und ihren Glanz behalten haben; so dass sie eher
neu gefärbt, als von Seewasser befleckt sind.

ANTONIO. Wenn nur eine von seinen Taschen sprechen könnte, würde
sie ihn nicht Lügen strafen?

SEBASTIAN. Ja, oder seine Aussage heuchlerischer Weise einstecken.

GONZALO. Mir deucht, unsre Kleider sind jetzt so frisch, als da wir sie zuerst in Afrika, bei der Heirat der schönen Tochter des Königs, Claribella,
mit dem König von Tunis, anlegten.

SEBASTIAN. Es war eine schöne Heirat, und wir haben viel Segen bei
unsrer Rückreise.

ADRIAN. Tunis war noch nie vorher mit solch einem Ausbunde von einer
Königin beglückt.

GONZALO. Seit den Zeiten der Witwe Dido nicht.

ANTONIO. Witwe? Hol's der Henker! Was hat die Witwe hier zu tun?
Witwe Dido?

SEBASTIAN. Wie, wenn er auch Witwer Äneas gesagt hätte? Lieber Himmel, wie Ihr gleich auffahrt!

ADRIAN. Witwe Dido, sagt Ihr? Ihr gebt mir da was zu denken: sie war ja
von Karthago, nicht von Tunis.

GONZALO. Dies Tunis, Herr, war Karthago.

ADRIAN. Karthago?

GONZALO. Ich versichre Euch, Karthago.

ANTONIO. Sein Wort vermag mehr als die wundertätige Harfe.

SEBASTIAN. He hath rais'd the wall, and houses too.

ANTONIO. What impossible matter will he make easy next?

SEBASTIAN. I think he will carry this island home in his pocket, and give it his son for an apple.

ANTONIO. And sowing the kernels of it in the sea, bring forth more islands.

GONZALO. Ay.

ANTONIO. Why, in good time.

GONZALO. Sir, we were talking that our garments seem now as fresh as when we were at Tunis at the marriage of your daughter, who is now queen.

ANTONIO. And the rarest that e'er came there.

SEBASTIAN. Bate, I beseech you, widow Dido.

ANTONIO. O, widow Dido? Ay, widow Dido.

GONZALO. Is not, sir, my doublet as fresh as the first day I wore it? I mean, in a sort.

ANTONIO. That ›sort‹ was well fish'd for.

GONZALO. When I wore it at your daughter's marriage?

ALONSO. You cram these words into mine ears against
The stomach of my sense. Would I had never
Married my daughter there! for coming thence,
My son is lost and (in my rate) she too,
Who is so far from Italy removed
I ne'er again shall see her. O thou mine heir
Of Naples and of Milan, what strange fish
Hath made his meal on thee?

FRANCISCO. Sir, he may live.
I saw him beat the surges under him,
And ride upon their backs. He trod the water,
Whose enmity he flung aside, and breasted
The surge most swoll'n that met him. His bold head
'Bove the contentious waves he kept, and oared
Himself with his good arms in lusty stroke
To th' shore, that o'er his wave-worn basis bowed,
As stooping to relieve him. I not doubt
He came alive to land.

ALONSO. No, no, he's gone.

SEBASTIAN. Sir, you may thank yourself for this great loss,
That would not bless our Europe with your daughter,
But rather loose her to an African,
Where she, at least, is banish'd from your eye,
Who hath cause to wet the grief on't.

ALONSO. Prithee peace.

SEBASTIAN. Er hat die Mauer aufgebaut und Häuser dazu.

ANTONIO. Welch eine Unmöglichkeit wird er zunächst zustande bringen?

SEBASTIAN. Ich denke, er trägt die Insel in der Tasche nach Haus und bringt sie seinem Sohn als einen Apfel mit.

ANTONIO. Und säet die Kerne davon in die See, um mehr Inseln zu ziehn.

GONZALO. Wie?

ANTONIO. Nun, weiter nichts.

GONZALO. Herr, wir sprachen davon, dass unsre Kleider jetzt noch so frisch aussehn, als da wir in Tunis bei der Vermählung Eurer Tochter waren, die nun Königin ist.

ANTONIO. Und zwar die herrlichste, die je dahin kam.

SEBASTIAN. Mit Erlaubnis, bis auf Witwe Dido.

ANTONIO. Oh, Witwe Dido! Ja, Witwe Dido.

GONZALO. Ist mein Wams nicht so frisch, Herr, als den ersten Tag, da ich es trug? Ich will sagen, auf gewisse Weise.

ANTONIO. Die Weise hat er zu rechter Zeit aufgefischt.

GONZALO. Da ich es bei der Vermählung Eurer Tochter trug?

ALONSO. Ihr stopft mir diese Wort' ins Ohr, ganz wider
Die Neigung meines Sinns. Hätt' ich doch nie
Die Tochter dort vermählt! Denn auf der Heimkehr
Verlor ich meinen Sohn; in meinen Augen
Auch sie, die so entfernt ist, dass ich nie
Sie werde wieder sehn. O du, mein Erbe
Von Napel und von Mailand, welcher Meerfisch
Hat dich verschlungen?

FRANCISCO. Herr, er lebt vielleicht.
Ich sah ihn unter sich die Wellen schlagen,
Auf ihrem Rücken reiten; er beschritt
Das Wasser, dessen Anfall von sich schleudernd,
Und bot die Brust der hochgeschwoll'nen Woge,
Die ihm entgegen kam. Das kühne Haupt
Hielt aus den streitbar'n Fluten er empor
Und ruderte sich selbst mit wackern Armen
In frischem Schlag ans Ufer, das zu ihm
Sich über seinen unterhöhlten Grund
Hinneigt', als wollt' es helfen: ohne Zweifel
Kam er gesund ans Land.

ALONSO. Nein, er ist hin.

SEBASTIAN. Herr, dankt Euch selber nur für den Verlust:
Ihr gönntet nicht Europa Eure Tochter,
Verlort sie an den Afrikaner lieber,
Wo sie verbannt doch lebt von Eurem Auge,
Das diesen Gram zu netzen Ursach' hat.

ALONSO. O still doch!

SEBASTIAN. You were kneel'd to, and importun'd otherwise
    By all of us, and the fair soul herself
    Weigh'd between loathness and obedience, at
    Which end o' th' beam should bow. We have lost your son,
    I fear for ever. Milan and Naples have
    Moe widows in them of this business' making
    Than we bring men to comfort them.
    The fault's your own.

ALONSO. So is the dear'st o' th' loss.
GONZALO. My Lord Sebastian,
    The truth you speak doth lack some gentleness,
    And time to speak it in. You rub the sore,
    When you should bring the plaster.
SEBASTIAN. Very well.
ANTONIO. And most chirurgeonly.
GONZALO. It is foul weather in us all, good sir,
    When you are cloudy.
SEBASTIAN. Fowl weather?
ANTONIO. Very foul.
GONZALO. Had I plantation of this isle, my lord –
ANTONIO. He'd sow't with nettle-seed.
SEBASTIAN. Or docks, or mallows.
GONZALO. And were the king on't, what would I do?
SEBASTIAN. Scape being drunk, for want of wine.
GONZALO. I' th' commonwealth I would, by contraries,
    Execute all things; for no kind of traffic
    Would I admit; no name of magistrate;
    Letters should not be known; riches, poverty,
    And use of service, none; contract, succession,
    Bourn, bound of land, tilth, vineyard, none;
    No use of metal, corn, or wine, or oil;
    No occupation, all men idle, all;
    And women too, but innocent and pure;
    No sovereignty –
SEBASTIAN. Yet he would be king on't.
ANTONIO. The latter end of his commonwealth forgets the beginning.
GONZALO. All things in common nature should produce
    Without sweat or endeavor: treason, felony,
    Sword, pike, knife, gun, or need of any engine,
    Would I not have; but nature should bring forth,
    Of it own kind, all foison, all abundance,
    To feed my innocent people.
SEBASTIAN. No marrying 'mong his subjects?

SEBASTIAN. Wir alle knieten und bestürmten Euch
    Vielfältig, und die holde Seele selbst
    Wog, zwischen Abscheu und Gehorsam, wo
    Die Schale sinken sollte. Euern Sohn
    Verloren wir für immer, wie ich fürchte.
    Mailand und Napel hat der Witwen mehr,
    Die dieser Handel machte, als wir Männer,
    Um sie zu trösten, bringen; und die Schuld
    Ist Euer.
ALONSO. Auch das Schwerste des Verlustes.
GONZALO. Mein Prinz Sebastian,
    Der Wahrheit, die Ihr sagt, fehlt etwas Milde
    Und die gelegne Zeit: Ihr reibt den Schaden,
    Statt Pflaster aufzulegen.
SEBASTIAN. Gut gesagt!
ANTONIO. Und sehr feldscherermäßig.
GONZALO. Es ist schlecht Wetter bei uns allen, Herr,
    Wenn Ihr betrübt seid.
SEBASTIAN. Schlecht Wetter?
ANTONIO. Sehr schlecht.
GONZALO. Hätt' ich, mein Fürst, die Pflanzung dieser Insel –
ANTONIO. Er säte Nesseln drauf.
SEBASTIAN. Oder Kletten, oder Malven.
GONZALO. Und wäre König hier: was würd' ich tun?
SEBASTIAN. Dem Trunk entgehn, weil er keinen Wein hätte.
GONZALO. Ich wirkte im gemeinen Wesen alles
    Durchs Gegenteil; denn keine Art von Handel
    Erlaubt' ich, keinen Namen eines Amts;
    Gelehrtheit sollte man nicht kennen; Reichtum,
    Dienst, Armut gäb's nicht; von Vertrag und Erbschaft,
    Verzäunung, Landmark, Feld- und Weinbau nichts;
    Auch kein Gebrauch von Korn, Wein, Öl, Metall,
    Kein Handwerk; alle Männer müßig, alle;
    Die Weiber auch, doch völlig rein und schuldlos;
    Kein Regiment –
SEBASTIAN. Und doch wollte er König sein!
ANTONIO. Das Ende seines gemeinen Wesens vergisst den Anfang.
GONZALO. In der gemeinsamen Natur sollt' alles
    Frucht bringen ohne Müh' und Schweiß; Verrat, Betrug,
    Schwert, Speer, Geschütz, Notwendigkeit der Waffen
    Gäb's nicht bei mir; es schaffte die Natur
    Von freien Stücken alle Hüll' und Fülle,
    Mein schuldlos Volk zu nähren.
SEBASTIAN. Keine Heiraten zwischen seinen Untertanen?

ANTONIO. None, man, all idle – whores and knaves.

GONZALO. I would with such perfection govern, sir,
  T' excel the golden age.
SEBASTIAN. 'Save his Majesty!
ANTONIO. Long live Gonzalo!
GONZALO. And – do you mark me, sir?
ALONSO. Prithee no more; thou dost talk nothing to me.
GONZALO. I do well believe your Highness, and did it to minister occa-
  sion to these gentlemen, who are of such sensible and nimble lungs that
  they always use to laugh at nothing.
ANTONIO. 'Twas you we laugh'd at.
GONZALO. Who, in this kind of merry fooling, am nothing to you; so
  you may continue, and laugh at nothing still.
ANTONIO. What a blow was there given!
SEBASTIAN. And it had not fall'n flat-long.
GONZALO. You are gentlemen of brave mettle; you would lift the moon
  out of her sphere, if she would continue in it five weeks without chan-
  ging.

Enter Ariel invisible, playing solemn music.

SEBASTIAN. We would so, and then go a-batfowling.

ANTONIO. Nay, good my lord, be not angry.
GONZALO. No, I warrant you, I will not adventure my discretion so
  weakly. Will you laugh me asleep, for I am very heavy?

ANTONIO. Go sleep, and hear us.

All sleep except Alonso, Sebastian, and Antonio.

ALONSO. What, all so soon asleep! I wish mine eyes
  Would, with themselves, shut up my thoughts. I find
  They are inclin'd to do so.
SEBASTIAN. Please you, sir,
  Do not omit the heavy offer of it.
  It seldom visits sorrow; when it doth,
  It is a comforter.
ANTONIO. We two, my lord,
  Will guard your person while you take your rest,
  And watch your safety.
ALONSO. Thank you. Wondrous heavy.

Alonso sleeps. Exit Ariel.

SEBASTIAN. What a strange drowsiness possesses them!
ANTONIO. It is the quality o' th' climate.

ANTONIO. Nichts dergleichen, Freund: alle los und ledig, Huren und
Taugenichtse.
GONZALO. So ungemein wollt' ich regieren, Herr,
Dass es die goldne Zeit verdunkeln sollte.
SEBASTIAN. Gott erhalte Seine Majestät!
ANTONIO. Lang' lebe Gonzalo!
GONZALO. Und – Ihr versteht mich, Herr?
ALONSO. Ich bitt' dich, schweig'! Du sprichst von Nichts zu mir.
GONZALO. Das glaube ich Eurer Hoheit gern; und ich tat es, um diesen
Herrn Gelegenheit zu machen, die so reizbare, bewegliche Lungen ha-
ben, dass sie immer über nichts zu lachen pflegen.
ANTONIO. Wir lachten über Euch.
GONZALO. Der ich in dieser Art von lustigen Possen gegen Euch nichts
bin; Ihr mögt daher fortfahren und ferner über nichts lachen.
ANTONIO. Was ward da für ein Streich versetzt!
SEBASTIAN. Ja, wenn er nicht flach gefallen wäre.
GONZALO. Ihr seid Kavaliere von herzhaftem Gemüt: Ihr würdet den
Mond aus seiner Sphäre heben, wenn er fünf Wochen darin bleiben
wollte, ohne zu wechseln.

Ariel kommt, unsichtbar, und spielt eine feierliche Melodie.

SEBASTIAN. Ja, das würden wir, und dann mit ihm ein Klopfjagen bei
Nacht anstellen.
ANTONIO. Lieber Herr, seid nicht ungehalten!
GONZALO. Nein, verlasst Euch drauf, ich werde meine Vernunft nicht so
leichtsinnig dran wagen. Wollt Ihr mich in Schlaf lachen, denn ich bin
sehr müde?
ANTONIO. Geht schlafen und hört uns zu!

Alle schlafen ein, außer Alonso, Sebastian und Antonio.

ALONSO. Wie? All' im Schlaf? O schlössen meine Augen
Mit sich auch die Gedanken zu! Ich fühle,
Sie sind dazu geneigt.
SEBASTIAN. Beliebt's Euch, Herr,
Versäumet nicht die müde Einladung.
Sie naht dem Kummer selten: wann sie's tut,
So bringt sie Trost.
ANTONIO. Wir beide wollen Euch
Behüten, gnäd'ger Herr, indes Ihr ruht,
Und Wache halten.
ALONSO. Dank Euch! Seltsam müde –

Alonso schläft ein. Ariel ab.

SEBASTIAN. Welch eine fremde Schläfrigkeit befällt sie?
ANTONIO. Es ist die Art des Himmelstrichs.

SEBASTIAN. Why
    Doth it not then our eyelids sink? I find not
    Myself dispos'd to sleep.
ANTONIO. Nor I, my spirits are nimble.
    They fell together all, as by consent;
    They dropp'd, as by a thunder-stroke. What might,
    Worthy Sebastian, O, what might –? No more –
    And yet methinks I see it in thy face,
    What thou shouldst be. Th' occasion speaks thee, and
    My strong imagination sees a crown
    Dropping upon thy head.
SEBASTIAN. What? art thou waking?
ANTONIO. Do you not hear me speak?
SEBASTIAN. I do, and surely
    It is a sleepy language, and thou speak'st
    Out of thy sleep. What is it thou didst say?
    This is a strange repose, to be asleep
    With eyes wide open – standing, speaking, moving –
    And yet so fast asleep.
ANTONIO. Noble Sebastian,
    Thou let'st thy fortune sleep – die, rather; wink'st
    Whiles thou art waking.
SEBASTIAN. Thou dost snore distinctly,
    There's meaning in thy snores.
ANTONIO. I am more serious than my custom; you
    Must be so too, if heed me; which to do,
    Trebles thee o'er.
SEBASTIAN. Well; I am standing water.
ANTONIO. I'll teach you how to flow.
SEBASTIAN. Do so. To ebb
    Hereditary sloth instructs me.
ANTONIO. O!
    If you but knew how you the purpose cherish
    Whiles thus you mock it! how, in stripping it,
    You more invest it! Ebbing men, indeed,
    Most often, do so near the bottom run
    By their own fear or sloth.
SEBASTIAN. Prithee say on.
    The setting of thine eye and cheek proclaim
    A matter from thee; and a birth, indeed,
    Which throes thee much to yield.
ANTONIO. Thus, sir:
    Although this lord of weak remembrance, this
    Who shall be of as little memory
    When he is earth'd, hath here almost persuaded

SEBASTIAN. Warum
    Drückt sie denn unsre Augenlider nicht?
    Ich fühl' in mir zum Schlafen keinen Trieb.
ANTONIO. Auch ich nicht, meine Sinne sind ganz munter.
    Sie fielen alle wie auf einen Wink,
    Sie sanken, wie vom Blitz gerührt. Was könnte –
    Würd'ger Sebastian? – Oh, was könnte? – Still! –
    Und doch ist mir, ich säh' auf deiner Stirn,
    Was du verdienst; der Anlass ruft, und meine
    Lebend'ge Einbildung sieht eine Krone
    Sich senken auf dein Haupt.
SEBASTIAN. Wie? Bist du wach?
ANTONIO. Hörst du mich denn nicht reden?
SEBASTIAN. Ja, und wahrlich,
    's ist eine Träumersprache, und du sprichst
    Aus deinem Schlaf. Was war es, das du sagtest?
    Dies ist 'ne wunderbare Ruh', zu schlafen
    Mit offnen Augen, stehend, sprechend, gehend,
    Und doch so tief im Schlaf.
ANTONIO. Edler Sebastian,
    Du lässt dein Glück entschlafen, sterben; taumelst,
    Indessen du doch wachst.
SEBASTIAN. Du schnarchst verständlich;
    Dein Schnarchen hat Bedeutung.
ANTONIO. Ja, ich bin ernster, als ich pflege, Ihr
    Müsst's auch sein, wenn Ihr mich begreift; und das
    Verdreifacht dich.
SEBASTIAN. Wohl, ich bin steh'ndes Wasser.
ANTONIO. Ich will Euch fluten lehren.
SEBASTIAN. Tut das doch:
    Denn ebben heißt mich angeerbte Trägheit.
ANTONIO. Oh,
    Wüßtet Ihr, wie Ihr den Anschlag hegt,
    Da Ihr ihn höhnt, wie, da Ihr ihn entblößt,
    Ihr mehr ihn schmückt! Denn freilich, wer da ebbt,
    Muss häufig auf den Grund beinah' geraten
    Durch eigne Furcht und Trägheit.
SEBASTIAN. Fahre fort,
    Ich bitte dich: dein Blick und deine Wange
    Verkünden etwas; die Geburt, fürwahr,
    Macht große Wehen dir.
ANTONIO. So hört! Obschon
    Der an Erinn'rung schwache Herr da, dieser,
    Der auch nicht stärker im Gedächtnis sein wird,
    Wenn er beerdigt ist, den König hier

(For he's a spirit of persuasion, only
Professes to persuade) the King his son's alive,
'Tis as impossible that he's undrown'd,
As he that sleeps here swims.

SEBASTIAN. I have no hope
   That he's undrown'd.
ANTONIO. O, out of that no hope
   What great hope have you! No hope, that way, is
   Another way so high a hope that even
   Ambition cannot pierce a wink beyond,
   But doubt discovery there. Will you grant with me
   That Ferdinand is drown'd?
SEBASTIAN. He's gone.
ANTONIO. Then tell me,
   Who's the next heir of Naples?
SEBASTIAN. Claribel.
ANTONIO. She that is Queen of Tunis; she that dwells
   Ten leagues beyond man's life; she that from Naples
   Can have no note, unless the sun were post –
   The Man i' th' Moon's too slow – till new-born chins
   Be rough and razorable; she that from whom
   We all were sea-swallow'd, though some cast again
   (And by that destiny) to perform an act
   Whereof what's past is prologue, what to come
   In yours and my discharge.

SEBASTIAN. What stuff is this? How say you?
   'Tis true, my brother's daughter 's Queen of Tunis,
   So is she heir of Naples; 'twixt which regions
   There is some space.

ANTONIO. A space whose ev'ry cubit
   Seems to cry out, »How shall that Claribel
   Measure us back to Naples? Keep in Tunis,
   And let Sebastian wake.« Say this were death
   That now hath seiz'd them, why, they were no worse
   Than now they are. There be that can rule Naples
   As well as he that sleeps; lords that can prate
   As amply and unnecessarily
   As this Gonzalo; I myself could make
   A chough of as deep chat. O that you bore
   The mind that I do! what a sleep were this
   For your advancement! Do you understand me?

Fast überredet hat – er ist ein Geist
Der Überredung, gibt mit nichts sich ab
Als überreden – , dass sein Sohn noch lebe:
's ist so unmöglich, dass er nicht ertrank,
Als dass der schwimme, der hier schläft.
SEBASTIAN. Ich bin
Ganz ohne Hoffnung, dass er nicht ertrank.
ANTONIO. Aus diesem ohne Hoffnung, oh, was geht Euch
Für große Hoffnung auf! Hier ohne Hoffnung, ist
Auf andre Art so hohe Hoffnung, dass
Der Blick der Ehrsucht selbst nicht jenseits dringt
Und, was er dort entdeckt, bezweifeln muss.
Gebt Ihr mir zu, dass Ferdinand ertrunken?
SEBASTIAN. Ja, er ist hin.
ANTONIO. So sagt mir, wer ist denn
Der nächste Erbe Napels?
SEBASTIAN. Claribella.
ANTONIO. Sie, Königin von Tunis? Die am Ende
Der Welt wohnt? Die von Napel keine Zeitung
Erhalten kann, wofern die Sonne nicht
Als Bote liefe (denn zu langsam ist
Der Mann im Mond), bis neugeborne Kinne
Bebartet sind? Von der uns alle kommend
Die See verschlang, doch ein'ge wieder auswarf;
Und dadurch sie ersehn zu einer Handlung,
Wovon, was jetzt geschah, ein Vorspiel ist,
Doch uns das Künft'ge obliegt.
SEBASTIAN. Was für Zeug ist dies?
Was sagt Ihr? – Wahr ist's, meines Bruders Tochter
Ist Königin von Tunis, ebenfalls
Von Napel Erbin, zwischen welchen Ländern
Ein wenig Raum ist.
ANTONIO. Ja, ein Raum, wovon
Ein jeder Fußbreit auszurufen scheint:
»Wie soll die Claribella uns zurück
Nach Napel messen?« – Bleibe sie in Tunis,
Sebastian wach'! – Setzt, dies wär' der Tod,
Was jetzt sie überfallen: nun, sie wären
Nicht schlimmer dran als jetzt. Es gibt der Leute,
Die Napel wohl so gut, als der hier schläft,
Regieren würden; Herrn, die schwatzen können,
So weit ausholend und so unersprießlich
Wie der Gonzalo hier; ich könnte selbst
So elsterhaft wohl plaudern. Hättet Ihr

SEBASTIAN. Methinks I do.
ANTONIO. And how does your content
    Tender your own good fortune?
SEBASTIAN. I remember
    You did supplant your brother Prospero.
ANTONIO. True.
    And look how well my garments sit upon me,
    Much feater than before. My brother's servants
    Were then my fellows, now they are my men.

SEBASTIAN. But, for your conscience?
ANTONIO. Ay, sir; where lies that? If 'twere a kibe,
    'Twould put me to my slipper; but I feel not
    This deity in my bosom. Twenty consciences,
    That stand 'twixt me and Milan, candied be they,
    And melt ere they molest! Here lies your brother,
    No better than the earth he lies upon,
    If he were that which now he's like – that's dead,
    Whom I with this obedient steel, three inches of it,
    Can lay to bed for ever; whiles you, doing thus,
    To the perpetual wink for aye might put
    This ancient morsel, this Sir Prudence, who
    Should not upbraid our course. For all the rest,
    They'll take suggestion as a cat laps milk;
    They'll tell the clock to any business that
    We say befits the hour.

SEBASTIAN. Thy case, dear friend,
    Shall be my president: as thou got'st Milan,
    I'll come by Naples. Draw thy sword. One stroke
    Shall free thee from the tribute which thou payest,
    And I the King shall love thee.
ANTONIO. Draw together;
    And when I rear my hand, do you the like,
    To fall it on Gonzalo.
SEBASTIAN. O, but one word.

They talk apart. Enter Ariel invisible, with music and song.

ARIEL. My master through his art foresees the danger
    That you, his friend, are in, and sends me forth
    (For else his project dies) to keep them living.

Sings in Gonzalo's ear.

Doch meinen Sinn! Was für ein Schlaf wär' dies
Für Eure Standserhöhung! Ihr versteht mich?
SEBASTIAN. Mich dünket, ja.
ANTONIO. Und wie hegt Euer Beifall
Eu'r eignes gutes Glück?
SEBASTIAN. Es fällt mir bei,
Ihr stürztet Euern Bruder Prospero.
ANTONIO. Wahr!
Und seht, wie wohl mir meine Kleider sitzen,
Weit saubrer wie zuvor. Des Bruders Diener,
Die damals meine Kameraden waren,
Sind meine Leute jetzt.
SEBASTIAN. Doch Eu'r Gewissen?
ANTONIO. Ei, Herr, wo sitzt das? Wär's der Frost im Fuß,
Müsst' ich in Socken gehn; allein ich fühle
Die Gottheit nicht im Busen. Zehn Gewissen,
Die zwischen mir und Mailand stehn, sie möchten
Gefroren sein und auftaun, eh' sie mir
Beschwerlich fielen. Hier liegt Euer Bruder, –
Nicht besser als die Erd', auf der er liegt,
Wär' er, was jetzt er scheinet, nämlich tot,
Den ich mit diesem will'gen Stahl, drei Zoll davon,
Zu Bett auf immer legen kann; indes Ihr gleichfalls
Die alte Ware da, den Meister Klug,
In Ruh'stand setztet, der uns weiter nichts
Vorrücken sollte. All die andern nehmen
Eingebung an, wie Milch die Katze schleckt;
Sie zählen uns zu jedem Werk die Stunde,
Wozu wir sagen, es sei Zeit.
SEBASTIAN. Mein Freund,
Dein Fall zeigt mir den Weg: wie du zu Mailand,
Komm' ich zu Napel. Zieh dein Schwert! Ein Streich
Löst vom Tribut dich, den du zahlst; und ich,
Der König, will dir hold sein.
ANTONIO. Zieht mit mir,
Und heb' ich meine Hand, tut Ihr desgleichen,
Und nieder auf Gonzalo!
SEBASTIAN. Halt, noch ein Wort!

Sie unterreden sich leise. Ariel kommt unsichtbar mit Musik und Lied.

ARIEL. Mein Herr sieht die Gefahr durch seine Kunst,
Worin Ihr schwebt, sein Freund; und schickt mich aus,
Weil sein Entwurf sonst stirbt, die hier zu retten.

Er singt in Gonzalos Ohr.

While you here do snoring lie,
Open-ey'd conspiracy
    His time doth take.
If of life you keep a care,
Shake off slumber, and beware.
    Awake, awake!
ANTONIO. Then let us both be sudden.
GONZALO *waking.* Now, good angels
    Preserve the King!

Wakes Alonso.

ALONSO. Why, how now, ho! Awake? Why are you drawn?
    Wherefore this ghastly looking?
GONZALO. What's the matter?
SEBASTIAN. Whiles we stood here securing your repose,
    Even now, we heard a hollow burst of bellowing
    Like bulls, or rather lions. Did't not wake you?
    It strook mine ear most terribly.
ALONSO. I heard nothing.
ANTONIO. O, 'twas a din to fright a monster's ear,
    To make an earthquake; sure it was the roar
    Of a whole herd of lions.
ALONSO. Heard you this, Gonzalo?
GONZALO. Upon mine honor, sir, I heard a humming
    (And that a strange one too) which did awake me.
    I shak'd you, sir, and cried. As mine eyes open'd,
    I saw their weapons drawn. There was a noise,
    That's verily. 'Tis best we stand upon our guard,
    Or that we quit this place. Let's draw our weapons.
ALONSO. Lead off this ground, and let's make further search
    For my poor son.
GONZALO. Heavens keep him from these beasts!
    For he is sure i' th' island.

ALONSO. Lead away.
ARIEL *aside.* Prospero my lord shall know what I have done.
    So, King, go safely on to seek thy son.

Exeunt.

        Weil Ihr schnarchet, nimmt zur Tat
        Offnen Auges der Verrat
            Die Zeit in acht.
        Ist Euch Leben lieb und Blut:
        Rüttelt Euch, seid auf der Hut!
            Erwacht! Erwacht!
ANTONIO. So lasst uns beide schnell sein!
GONZALO *erwacht.* Ihr guten Engel,
    Steht dem König bei!

Alonso erwacht.

ALONSO. Wie? Was? He! wach? Wozu mit bloßem Degen?
    Warum die stieren Blicke?
GONZALO. Nun, was gibt's?
SEBASTIAN. Da wir hier standen, Eure Ruh' bewachend,
    Jetzt eben brach ein hohles Brüllen aus,
    Als wie von Bullen oder Löwen gar.
    Weckt' es Euch nicht? Es traf mein Ohr entsetzlich.
ALONSO. Ich hörte nichts.
ANTONIO. Oh, ein Getös', um Ungeheu'r zu schrecken,
    Erdbeben zu erregen! Das Gebrüll
    Von ganzen Herden Löwen!
ALONSO. Hörtet Ihr's, Gonzalo?
GONZALO. Auf meine Ehre, Herr, ich hört' ein Summen,
    Und zwar ein sonderbares, das mich weckte;
    Ich schüttelt' Euch und rief: als ich die Augen auftat,
    Sah ich die Degen bloß. Ein Lärm war da,
    Das ist gewiss: wir sollten auf der Hut sein
    Und diesen Platz verlassen. Zieht die Degen!
ALONSO. Gehn wir von hier, und lasst uns weiter suchen
    Nach meinem armen Sohn!
GONZALO. Behüt ihn Gott
    Vor diesen wilden Tieren! denn er ist
    Gewisslich auf der Insel.
ALONSO. Lasst uns gehn!
ARIEL *für sich.* Ich will, was ich getan, dem Meister offenbaren.
    Geh, König, such' den Sohn, nun sicher vor Gefahren!

Alle ab.

Scene II

Enter Caliban with a burthen of wood. A noise of thunder heard.

CALIBAN. All the infections that the sun sucks up
    From bogs, fens, flats, on Prosper fall, and make him
    By inch-meal a disease! His spirits hear me,
    And yet I needs must curse. But they'll nor pinch,
    Fright me with urchin-shows, pitch me i' th' mire,
    Nor lead me, like a fire-brand, in the dark
    Out of my way, unless he bid 'em; but
    For every trifle are they set upon me,
    Sometime like apes that mow and chatter at me,
    And after bite me; then like hedgehogs which
    Lie tumbling in my barefoot way, and mount
    Their pricks at my footfall; sometime am I
    All wound with adders, who with cloven tongues
    Do hiss me into madness.

Enter Trinculo.

    Lo, now lo,
    Here comes a spirit of his, and to torment me
    For bringing wood in slowly. I'll fall flat,
    Perchance he will not mind me.

TRINCULO. Here's neither bush nor shrub to bear off any weather at all. And another storm brewing, I hear it sing i' th' wind. Yond same black cloud, yond huge one, looks like a foul bumbard that would shed his liquor. If it should thunder as it did before, I know not where to hide my head. Yond same cloud cannot choose but fall by pailfuls. What have we here? a man or a fish? dead or alive? A fish, he smells like a fish; a very ancient and fish-like smell; a kind of, not-of-the-newest poor-John. A strange fish! Were I in England now (as once I was) and had but this fish painted, not a holiday fool there but would give a piece of silver. There would this monster make a man; any strange beast there makes a man. When they will not give a doit to relieve a lame beggar, they will lay out ten to see a dead Indian. Legg'd like a man; and his fins like arms! Warm, o' my troth! I do now let loose my opinion, hold it no longer: this is no fish, but an islander, that hath lately suffer'd by a thunderbolt. *Thunder.* Alas, the storm is come again! My best way is to creep under his gaberdine; there is no other shelter hereabout. Misery acquaints a man with strange bedfellows; I will here shroud till the dregs of the storm be past.

Zweite Szene

Caliban kommt mit einer Tracht Holz. Man hört in der Entfernung donnern.

CALIBAN. Dass aller Giftqualm, den die Sonn' aufsaugt
  Aus Sumpf, Moor, Pfuhl, auf Prosper fall' und mach' ihn
  Siech durch und durch! Mich hören seine Geister.
  Und muss doch fluchen. Zwar sie kneifen nicht,
  Erschrecken mich als Igel, stecken mich
  In Kot, noch führen sie wie Bränd' im Dunkeln
  Mich irre, wenn er's nicht geheißen; aber
  Für jeden Bettel hetzt er sie auf mich;
  Wie Affen bald, die Mäuler ziehn und plärren
  Und dann mich beißen; bald wie Stachelschweine,
  Die, wo ich barfuß geh', sich wälzen und
  Die Borsten sträuben, wenn mein Fuß auftritt;
  Manchmal bin ich von Nattern ganz umwunden,
  Die mit gespaltnen Zungen toll mich zischen.

Trinculo kommt.

  Seht! jetzt! Hu, hu! Da kommt ein Geist von ihm,
  Um mich zu plagen, weil ich's Holz nicht bringe;
  Platt fall' ich hin, so merkt er wohl mich nicht.

TRINCULO. Hier ist weder Busch noch Strauch, einen nur ein bisschen
vor dem Wetter zu schützen, und schon munkelt ein neues Ungewitter.
Ich hör's im Winde pfeifen: die schwarze Wolke da, die große, sieht wie
ein alter Schlauch aus, der sein Getränk verschütten will. Wenn es wieder
so donnert wie vorher, so weiß ich nicht, wo ich unterducken soll; die
Wolke da muss schlechterdings mit Mulden gießen. – Was gibt's hier?
Ein Mensch oder ein Fisch? Tot oder lebendig? Ein Fisch: er riecht wie
ein Fisch; 's ist ein recht ranziger und fischichter Geruch; so 'ne Art La-
berdan, nicht von dem frischesten. Ein seltsamer Fisch! Wenn ich nun
in England wäre, wie ich einmal gewesen bin, und hätte den Fisch nur
gemalt, jeder Pfingstnarr gäbe mir dort ein Stück Silber. Da wäre ich mit
dem Ungeheuer ein gemachter Mann; jedes fremde Tier macht dort seinen Mann; wenn sie keinen Deut geben wollen, einem lahmen Bettler zu
helfen, so wenden sie zehn dran, einen toten Indianer zu sehn. – Beine
wie ein Mensch! Seine Floßfedern wie Arme! Warm, mein' Seel'! Ich lasse
jetzt meine Meinung fahren und behaupte sie nicht länger: es ist kein
Fisch, sondern einer von der Insel, den ein Donnerkeil eben erschlagen
hat. *Donner.* O weh! das Ungewitter ist wieder heraufgekommen: das
beste ist, ich krieche unter seinen Mantel, es gibt hier herum kein andres
Obdach. Die Not bringt einen zu seltsamen Schlafgesellen; ich will mich
hier einwickeln, bis die Grundsuppe des Gewitters vorüber ist.

Enter Stephano, singing, a bottle in his hand.

STEPHANO.
>»I shall no more to sea, to sea,
>   Here shall I die ashore —«
> This is a very scurvy tune to sing at a man's funeral.
> Well, here's my comfort.

Drinks.

(Sings.)

>»The master, the swabber, the boatswain, and I,
>   The gunner and his mate,
> Lov'd Mall, Meg, and Marian, and Margery,
>   But none of us car'd for Kate;
>   For she had a tongue with a tang,
>   Would cry to a sailor, ›Go hang!‹
> She lov'd not the savor of tar nor of pitch,
> Yet a tailor might scratch her where e'er she did itch.
>   Then to sea, boys, and let her go hang!«
> This is a scurvy tune too; but here's my comfort.

Drinks.

CALIBAN. Do not torment me! O!

STEPHANO. What's the matter? Have we devils here? Do you put tricks upon 's with salvages and men of Inde? Ha? I have not scap'd drowning to be afeard now of your four legs; for it hath been said, »As proper a man as ever went on four legs cannot make him give ground«; and it shall be said so again while Stephano breathes at' nostrils.

CALIBAN. The spirit torments me! O!

STEPHANO. This is some monster of the isle with four legs, who hath got (as I take it) an ague. Where the devil should he learn our language? I will give him some relief, if it be but for that. If I can recover him, and keep him tame, and get to Naples with him, he's a present for any emperor that ever trod on neat's-leather.

CALIBAN. Do not torment me, prithee. I'll bring my wood home faster.

STEPHANO. He's in his fit now, and does not talk after the wisest. He shall taste of my bottle; if he have never drunk wine afore, it will go near to remove his fit. If I can recover him, and keep him tame, I will not take too much for him; he shall pay for him that hath him, and that soundly.

CALIBAN. Thou dost me yet but little hurt; thou wilt anon, I know it by thy trembling. Now Prosper works upon thee.

Stephano kommt singend, eine Flasche in der Hand.

STEPHANO.

>Ich geh' nicht mehr zur See, zur See,
>>Hier sterb' ich auf dem Land. –

Das ist eine lausige Melodie, gut bei einer Beerdigung zu singen:
Aber hier ist mein Trost.

Trinkt.

(Singt.)

>Der Meister, der Bootsmann, der Konstabel und ich,
>>Wir halten's mit artigen Mädchen,
>Mit Lieschen und Gretchen und Hedewig;
>>Doch keiner fragt was nach Käthchen.
>>Denn sie macht ein beständig Gekeifel;
>>Kommt ein Seemann, da heißt's: geh zum Teufel!
>Den Pech- und den Teergeruch hasst sie aufs Blut;
>Doch ein Schneider, der juckt sie, wo's nötig ihr tut,
>>Auf die See, Kerls, und hol' sie der Teufel!

Das ist auch eine lausige Melodie; aber hier ist mein Trost.

Trinkt.

CALIBAN. Plage mich nicht! Oh!

STEPHANO. Was heißt das? Gibt's hier Teufel! Habt ihr uns zum besten mit Wilden und indianischen Männern? Ha! Dazu bin ich nicht nahe am Ersaufen gewesen, um mich jetzt vor deinen vier Beinen zu fürchten; denn es heißt von ihm: so 'n wackrer Kerl, als jemals auf vier Beinen gegangen ist, kann ihn nicht zum Weichen bringen; und es soll auch ferner so heißen, solange Stephano einen lebendigen Odem in seiner Nase hat.

CALIBAN. Der Geist plagt mich – Oh! –

STEPHANO. Dies ist ein Ungeheuer aus der Insel mit vier Beinen, der meines Bedünkens das Fieber gekriegt hat. Wo Henker mag er unsre Sprache gelernt haben? Ich will ihm was zur Stärkung geben, wär's nur deswegen: kann ich ihn wieder zurecht bringen und ihn zahm machen, und nach Neapel mit ihm kommen, so ist er ein Präsent für den besten Kaiser, der je auf Rindsleder getreten ist.

CALIBAN. Plag' mich nicht, bitte! Ich will mein Holz geschwinder zu Haus bringen.

STEPHANO. Er hat jetzt seinen Anfall und redet nicht zum gescheitesten. Er soll aus meiner Flasche kosten; wenn er noch niemals Wein getrunken hat, so kann es ihm leicht das Fieber vertreiben. Kann ich ihn wieder zurecht bringen und ihn zahm machen, so will ich nicht zu viel für ihn nehmen: wer ihn kriegt, soll für ihn bezahlen, und das tüchtig.

CALIBAN. Noch tust du mir nicht viel zu Leid; du wirst es bald, ich merk's an deinem Zittern. Jetzt treibt dich Prospero.

STEPHANO. Come on your ways. Open your mouth; here is that which will give language to you, cat. Open your mouth; this will shake your shaking, I can tell you, and that soundly. You cannot tell who's your friend. Open your chaps again.

Caliban drinks.

TRINCULO. I should know that voice; it should be – but he is drown'd; and these are devils. O, defend me!
STEPHANO. Four legs and two voices; a most delicate monster! His forward voice now is to speak well of his friend; his backward voice is to utter foul speeches and to detract. If all the wine in my bottle will recover him, I will help his ague. Come. *Caliban drinks again.* Amen! I will pour some in thy other mouth.

TRINCULO. Stephano!
STEPHANO. Doth thy other mouth call me? Mercy, mercy! This is a devil, and no monster. I will leave him, I have no long spoon.

TRINCULO. Stephano! If thou beest Stephano, touch me, and speak to me; for I am Trinculo – be not afeard – thy good friend Trinculo.

STEPHANO. If thou beest Trinculo, come forth. I'll pull thee by the lesser legs. If any be Trinculo's legs, these are they. Thou art very Trinculo indeed! How cam'st thou to be the siege of this moon-calf? Can he vent Trinculos?

TRINCULO. I took him to be kill'd with a thunder-stroke. But art thou not drown'd, Stephano? I hope now thou art not drown'd. Is the storm overblown? I hid me under the dead moon-calf's gaberdine for fear of the storm. And art thou living, Stephano? O Stephano, two Neapolitans scap'd!
STEPHANO. Prithee do not turn me about, my stomach is not constant.
CALIBAN *aside.*
These be fine things, and if they be not sprites.
That's a brave god, and bears celestial liquor.
I will kneel to him.

STEPHANO. How didst thou scape? How cam'st thou hither? Swear by this bottle how thou cam'st hither – I escap'd upon a butt of sack which the sailors heav'd o'erboard – by this bottle, which I made of the bark of a tree with mine own hands since I was cast ashore.

CALIBAN. I'll swear upon that bottle to be thy true subject, for the liquor is not earthly.
STEPHANO. Here; swear then how thou escap'dst.

STEPHANO. Lass das gut sein! Mach' das Maul auf! Hier ist was, das dich zur Vernunft bringen soll, Katze: mach' das Maul auf! Dies wird dein Schütteln schütteln, sag' ich dir, und das tüchtig. Niemand weiß, wer sein Freund ist. Tu' die Kinnbacken wieder auf!

Caliban drinkt.

TRINCULO. Ich sollte die Stimme kennen; das wäre ja wohl – aber er ist ertrunken, und dies sind Teufel. Oh, behüte mich!

STEPHANO. Vier Beine und zwei Stimmen: ein allerliebstes Ungeheuer! Seine Vorderstimme wird nun Gutes von seinem Freunde reden; seine Hinterstimme wird böse Reden ausstoßen und verleumden. Reicht der Wein in meiner Flasche hin, ihn zurecht zu bringen, so will ich sein Fieber kurieren. Komm! *Caliban trinkt erneut.* Amen! Ich will dir was in deinen andern Mund gießen.

TRINCULO. Stephano –

STEPHANO. Ruft mich dein andrer Mund bei Namen? Behüte! Behüte! Dies ist der Teufel und kein Ungeheuer. Ich will keine Suppe mit ihm essen, ich habe keinen langen Löffel.

TRINCULO. Stephano! – Wenn du Stephano bist, rühr' mich an und sprich mit mir, denn ich bin Trinculo – fürchte dich nicht! – dein guter Freund Trinculo.

STEPHANO. Wenn du Trinculo bist, so komm heraus! Ich will dich bei den dünneren Beinen ziehen: wenn hier welche Trinculos Beine sind, so sind's diese. – Du bist wirklich ganz und gar Trinculo. Wie kamst du dazu, der Abgang dieses Mondkalbes zu sein? Kann er Trinculos von sich geben?

TRINCULO. Ich dachte, er wäre vom Blitz erschlagen. – Bist du denn nicht ertrunken, Stephano? Ich will hoffen, du bist nicht ertrunken. Ist das Ungewitter vorüber? Ich steckte mich unter des toten Mondkalbes Mantel, weil ich vor dem Ungewitter bange war. Du bist also am Leben, Stephano? O Stephano, zwei Neapolitaner davon gekommen!

STEPHANO. Ich bitte dich, dreh' mich nicht so herum, mein Magen ist nicht recht standfest.

CALIBAN *beiseite.*
Gar schöne Dinger, wo's nicht Geister sind!
Das ist ein wackrer Gott, hat Himmelstrank:
Will vor ihm knien.

STEPHANO. Wie kamst du davon? Wie kamst du hierher? Schwöre bei dieser Flasche, wie du herkamst. Ich habe mich auf einem Fasse Sekt gerettet, das die Matrosen über Bord warfen: bei dieser Flasche, die ich aus Baumrinden mit meinen eignen Händen gemacht habe, seit ich ans Land getrieben bin!

CALIBAN. Bei der Flasche will ich schwören, dein treuer Knecht zu sein, denn das ist kein irdisches Getränk.

STEPHANO. Hier schwöre nun: wie kamst du ans Land?

TRINCULO. Sworn ashore, man, like a duck. I can swim like a duck, I'll
    be sworn.
STEPHANO. Here, kiss the book. *Passing the bottle.* Though thou canst
    swim like a duck, thou art made like a goose.
TRINCULO. O Stephano, hast any more of this?
STEPHANO. The whole butt, man. My cellar is in a rock by th' sea-side,
    where my wine is hid. How now, moon-calf? how does thine ague?

CALIBAN. Hast thou not dropp'd from heaven?
STEPHANO. Out o' th' moon, I do assure thee. I was the Man i' th'
    Moon, when time was.
CALIBAN. I have seen thee in her, and I do adore thee. My mistress
    show'd me thee, and thy dog, and thy bush.
STEPHANO. Come, swear to that; kiss the book. I will furnish it anon
    with new contents. Swear.

Caliban drinks.

TRINCULO. By this good light, this is a very shallow monster! I afeard of
    him? A very weak monster! The Man i' th' Moon? A most poor credulous
    monster! Well drawn, monster, in good sooth!

CALIBAN. I'll show thee every fertile inch o' th' island;
    And I will kiss thy foot. I prithee be my god.
TRINCULO. By this light, a most perfidious and drunken monster! When
    's god's asleep, he'll rob his bottle.
CALIBAN. I'll kiss thy foot. I'll swear myself thy subject.

STEPHANO. Come on then; down, and swear.
TRINCULO. I shall laugh myself to death at this puppy-headed monster.
    A most scurvy monster! I could find in my heart to beat him –
STEPHANO. Come, kiss.
TRINCULO. But that the poor monster's in drink. An abominable mons-
    ter!
CALIBAN. I'll show thee the best springs; I'll pluck thee berries;
    I'll fish for thee, and get thee wood enough.
    A plague upon the tyrant that I serve!
    I'll bear him no more sticks, but follow thee,
    Thou wondrous man.
TRINCULO. A most ridiculous monster, to make a wonder of a poor
    drunkard!
CALIBAN. I prithee let me bring thee where crabs grow;
    And I with my long nails will dig thee pig-nuts,
    Show thee a jay's nest, and instruct thee how
    To snare the nimble marmazet. I'll bring thee
    To clust'ring filberts, and sometimes I'll get thee
    Young scamels from the rock. Wilt thou go with me?

TRINCULO. Ans Land geschwommen, Kerl, wie 'ne Ente; ich kann schwimmen wie 'ne Ente, das schwör' ich dir.

STEPHANO. Hier küsse das Buch! *Passiert die Flasche.* Kannst du schon schwimmen wie 'ne Ente, so bist du doch natürlich wie eine Gans.

TRINCULO. O Stephano, hast mehr davon?

STEPHANO. Das ganze Fass, Kerl; mein Keller ist in einem Felsen an der See, da habe ich meinen Wein versteckt. Nun, Mondkalb? was macht dein Fieber?

CALIBAN. Bist du nicht vom Himmel gefallen?

STEPHANO. Ja, aus dem Monde, glaub's mir: ich war zu seiner Zeit der Mann im Monde.

CALIBAN. Ich habe dich drin gesehn und bete dich an. Meine Gebieterin zeigte dich mir und deinen Hund und deinen Busch.

STEPHANO. Komm, schwöre hierauf! Küsse das Buch! Ich will es gleich mit neuem Inhalt anfüllen! Schwöre!

Caliban trinkt.

TRINCULO. Beim Firmament, das ist ein recht einfältiges Ungeheuer. – Ich mich vor ihm fürchten? – Ein recht betrübtes Ungeheuer! Der Mann im Monde? – Ein armes leichtgläubiges Ungeheuer! – Gut ausgedacht, Ungeheuer, meiner Treu!

CALIBAN. Ich zeig' dir jeden fruchtbar'n Fleck der Insel
Und will den Fuß dir küssen: bitte, sei mein Gott!

TRINCULO. Beim Firmament, ein recht hinterlistiges betrunknes Ungeheuer! Wenn sein Gott schläft, wird es ihm die Flasche stehlen.

CALIBAN. Ich will den Fuß dir küssen, will mich schwören zu deinem Knecht.

STEPHANO. So komm denn: nieder, und schwöre!

TRINCULO. Ich lache mich zu Tode über dies mopsköpfige Ungeheuer. Ein lausiges Ungeheuer! Ich könnte über mich gewinnen, es zu prügeln. –

STEPHANO. Komm! küss!

TRINCULO. Wenn das arme Ungeheuer nicht besoffen wäre. – Ein abscheuliches Ungeheuer!

CALIBAN. Will dir die Quellen zeigen, Beeren pflücken,
Will fischen und dir Holz genügsam schaffen.
Pest dem Tyrannen, dem ich dienen muss!
Ich trag' ihm keine Klötze mehr; ich folge
Dir nach, du Wundermann.

TRINCULO. Ein lächerliches Ungeheuer, aus einem armen Trunkenbolde ein Wunder zu machen.

CALIBAN. Lass mich dir weisen, wo die Holzbirn' wächst;
Mit meinen langen Nägeln grab' ich Trüffeln,
Zeig' dir des Hähers Nest; ich lehre dich,
Die hurt'ge Meerkatz' fangen; bringe dich
Zum vollen Haselbusch und hol' dir manchmal
Vom Felsen junge Möwen. Willst du mitgehn?

STEPHANO. I prithee now lead the way without any more talking.
  Trinculo, the King and all our company else being drown'd, we will
  inherit here. Here! bear my bottle. Fellow Trinculo, we'll fill him by and
  by again.
CALIBAN *sings drunkenly.*
  Farewell, master; farewell, farewell!
TRINCULO. A howling monster; a drunken monster!
CALIBAN.
        No more dams I'll make for fish,
            Nor fetch in firing
            At requiring,
        Nor scrape trenchering, nor wash dish.
            'Ban, 'Ban, Ca-Caliban
        Has a new master, get a new man.
        Freedom, high-day! high-day, freedom! freedom, high-day, free-
        dom!
STEPHANO. O brave monster! lead the way.

Exeunt.

Act III
Scene I

Enter Ferdinand bearing a log.

FERDINAND. There be some sports are painful, and their labor
  Delight in them sets off; some kinds of baseness
  Are nobly undergone; and most poor matters
  Point to rich ends. This my mean task
  Would be as heavy to me as odious, but
  The mistress which I serve quickens what's dead,
  And makes my labors pleasures. O, she is
  Ten times more gentle than her father's crabbed;
  And he's compos'd of harshness. I must remove
  Some thousands of these logs, and pile them up,
  Upon a sore injunction. My sweet mistress
  Weeps when she sees me work, and says such baseness
  Had never like executor. I forget;
  But these sweet thoughts do even refresh my labors,
  Most busil'est when I do it.

Enter Miranda, and Prospero at a distance, unseen.

STEPHANO. Ich bitte dich, geh voran, ohne weiter zu schwatzen. – Trinculo, da der König und unsre ganze Mannschaft ertrunken ist, so wollen wir hier Besitz nehmen. – Hier, trag‘ meine Flasche! – Kamerad Trinculo, wir wollen sie gleich wieder füllen.

CALIBAN *singt im betrunknen Mute.*
Leb wohl, mein Meister! Leb wohl! leb wohl!

TRINCULO. Ein heulendes Ungeheuer! ein besoffenes Ungeheuer!

CALIBAN.
Will nicht mehr Fischfänger sein,
    Noch Feu‘rung holen,
    Wie‘s befohlen;
Noch die Teller scheuern rein:
    Ban, ban, Ca – Caliban
Hat zum Herrn einen andern Mann:
Schaff einen neuen Diener dir an!
Freiheit, heisa! heisa, Freiheit! Freiheit, heisa! Freiheit!

STEPHANO. O tapfres Ungeheuer, zeig‘ uns den Weg!

Alle ab.

Dritter Aufzug
Erste Szene

Ferdinand, ein Scheit Holz tragend.

FERDINAND. Es gibt müh‘volle Spiele, und die Arbeit
Erhöht die Lust dran; mancher schnöde Dienst
Wird rühmlich übernommen, und das Ärmste
Führt zu dem reichsten Ziel. Dies niedre Tagwerk
Wär‘ so beschwerlich als verhasst mir; doch
Die Herrin, der ich dien‘, erweckt das Tote
Und macht die Müh‘n zu Freuden. Oh, sie ist
Zehnfach so freundlich als ihr Vater rau,
Und er besteht aus Härte. Schleppen muss ich
Und schichten ein paar tausend dieser Klötze,
Bei schwerer Strafe: meine süße Herrin
Weint, wenn sie‘s sieht, und sagt, so knecht‘scher Dienst
Fand nimmer solchen Täter. Ich vergesse;
Doch diese lieblichen Gedanken laben
Die Arbeit selbst; ich bin am müßigsten,
Wann ich sie tue.

Miranda kommt. Prospero in einiger Entfernung ungesehen.

MIRANDA. Alas, now pray you
    Work not so hard. I would the lightning had
    Burnt up those logs that you are enjoin‘d to pile!
    Pray set it down, and rest you. When this burns,
    'Twill weep for having wearied you. My father
    Is hard at study; pray now rest yourself,
    He‘s safe for these three hours.
FERDINAND. O most dear mistress,
    The sun will set before I shall discharge
    What I must strive to do.
MIRANDA. If you‘ll sit down,
    I‘ll bear your logs the while. Pray give me that,
    I‘ll carry it to the pile.
FERDINAND. No, precious creature,
    I had rather crack my sinews, break my back,
    Than you should such dishonor undergo,
    While I sit lazy by.
MIRANDA. It would become me
    As well as it does you; and I should do it
    With much more ease, for my good will is to it,
    And yours it is against.
PROSPERO *aside*. Poor worm, thou art infected!
    This visitation shows it.
MIRANDA. You look wearily.
FERDINAND. No, noble mistress, 'tis fresh morning with me
    When you are by at night. I do beseech you –
    Chiefly that I might set it in my prayers –
    What is your name?

MIRANDA. Miranda. – O my father,
    I have broke your hest to say so.
FERDINAND. Admir‘d Miranda,
    Indeed the top of admiration! worth
    What‘s dearest to the world! Full many a lady
    I have ey‘d with best regard, and many a time
    Th‘ harmony of their tongues hath into bondage
    Brought my too diligent ear. For several virtues
    Have I lik‘d several women, never any
    With so full soul but some defect in her
    Did quarrel with the noblest grace she ow‘d,
    And put it to the foil. But you, O you,
    So perfect and so peerless, are created
    Of every creature‘s best!
 MIRANDA. I do not know
    One of my sex; no woman‘s face remember,

MIRANDA. Ach, ich bitte, plagt
    Euch nicht so sehr! Ich wollte, dass der Blitz
    Das Holz verbrannt, das Ihr zu schichten habt.
    Legt ab und ruht Euch aus! Wenn dies hier brennt,
    Wird's weinen, dass es Euch beschwert. Mein Vater
    Steckt tief in Büchern: Bitte, ruht Euch aus!
    Ihr seid vor ihm jetzt auf drei Stunden sicher.
FERDINAND. O teuerste Gebieterin! die Sonne
    Wird untergehn, eh' ich vollbringen kann,
    Was ich doch muss.
MIRANDA. Wenn Ihr Euch setzen wollt,
    Trag' ich indes die Klötze. Gebt mir den!
    Ich bring' ihn hin.
FERDINAND. Nein, köstliches Geschöpf!
    Eh' sprengt' ich meine Sehnen, bräch' den Rücken,
    Als dass Ihr solcher Schmach Euch unterzögt,
    Und ich säh' träge zu.
MIRANDA. Es stände mir
    So gut wie Euch, und ich verrichtet' es
    Weit leichter, denn mich treibt mein guter Wille,
    Und Euerm ist's zuwider.
PROSPERO *beiseite*. Armer Wurm,
    Du bist gefangen! Dein Besuch verrät's.
MIRANDA. Ihr seht ermüdet aus.
FERDINAND. Nein, edle Herrin,
    Bei mir ist's früher Morgen, wenn Ihr mir
    Am Abend nah seid. Ich ersuche Euch
    Hauptsächlich, um Euch im Gebet zu nennen,
    Wie heißet Ihr?
MIRANDA. Miranda. – O mein Vater!
    Ich hab' Eu'r Wort gebrochen, da ich's sagte.
FERDINAND. Bewunderte Miranda! In der Tat
    Der Gipfel der Bewund'rung; was die Welt
    Am höchsten achtet, wert! Gar manches Fräulein
    Betrachtet' ich mit Fleiß, und manches Mal
    Bracht' ihrer Zungen Harmonie in Knechtschaft
    Mein allzu emsig Ohr; um andre Gaben
    Gefielen andre Frau'n mir; keine je
    So ganz von Herzen, dass ein Fehl in ihr
    Nicht haderte mit ihrem schönsten Reiz
    Und überwältigt' ihn: doch Ihr, oh, Ihr,
    So ohnegleichen, so vollkommen, seid
    Vom besten jegliches Geschöpfs erschaffen.
MIRANDA. Vom eigenen Geschlechte kenn' ich niemand,
    Erinn're mir kein weibliches Gesicht,

Save, from my glass, mine own; nor have I seen
More that I may call men than you, good friend,
And my dear father. How features are abroad
I am skilless of; but by my modesty
(The jewel in my dower), I would not wish
Any companion in the world but you;
Nor can imagination form a shape,
Besides yourself, to like of. But I prattle
Something too wildly, and my father's precepts
I therein do forget.

FERDINAND. I am, in my condition,
A prince, Miranda; I do think, a king
(I would, not so!), and would no more endure
This wooden slavery than to suffer
The flesh-fly blow my mouth. Hear my soul speak:
The very instant that I saw you, did
My heart fly to your service, there resides,
To make me slave to it, and for your sake
Am I this patient log-man.

MIRANDA. Do you love me?
FERDINAND. O heaven, O earth, bear witness to this sound,
And crown what I profess with kind event
If I speak true! if hollowly, invert
What best is boded me to mischief! I,
Beyond all limit of what else i' th' world,
Do love, prize, honor you.
MIRANDA. I am a fool
To weep at what I am glad of.
PROSPERO *aside*. Fair encounter
Of two most rare affections! Heavens rain grace
On that which breeds between 'em!
FERDINAND. Wherefore weep you?
MIRANDA. At mine unworthiness, that dare not offer
What I desire to give; and much less take
What I shall die to want. But this is trifling,
And all the more it seeks to hide itself,
The bigger bulk it shows. Hence, bashful cunning,
And prompt me, plain and holy innocence!
I am your wife, if you will marry me;
If not, I'll die your maid. To be your fellow
You may deny me, but I'll be your servant,
Whether you will or no.

Als meines nur im Spiegel; und ich sah
Nicht mehre, die ich Männer nennen könnte,
Als Euch, mein Guter, und den teuern Vater.
Was für Gesichter anderswo es gibt,
Ist unbewusst mir; doch bei meiner Sittsamkeit,
Dem Kleinod meiner Mitgift! wünsch' ich keinen
Mir zum Gefährten in der Welt als Euch,
Noch kann die Einbildung ein Wesen schaffen,
Das ihr gefiele, außer Euch. Allein
Ich plaudre gar zu wild und achte darin
Des Vaters Vorschrift nicht.
FERDINAND. Ich bin nach meinem Stand
Ein Prinz, Miranda, ja ich denk', ein König –
(Wär' ich's doch nicht!), – und trüg' so wenig wohl
Hier diese hölzerne Leibeigenschaft,
Als ich von einer Fliege mir den Mund
Zerstechen ließ'. – Hört meine Seele reden!
Den Augenblick, da ich Euch sahe, flog
Mein Herz in Euern Dienst; da wohnt es nun,
Um mich zum Knecht zu machen: Euretwegen
Bin ich ein so geduld'ger Tagelöhner.
MIRANDA. Liebt Ihr mich?
FERDINAND. O Erd', o Himmel! zeuget diesem Laut
Und krönt mit günst'gem Glück, was ich beteure,
Red' ich die Wahrheit; red' ich falsch, so kehrt
Die beste Vorbedeutung mir in Unglück!
Weit über alles, was die Welt sonst hat,
Lieb' ich und acht' und ehr' Euch.
MIRANDA. Ich bin töricht,
Zu weinen über etwas, das mich freut.
PROSPERO *beiseite*. Ein schön Begegnen zwei erwählter Herzen!
Der Himmel regne Huld auf das herab,
Was zwischen ihnen aufkeimt!
FERDINAND. Warum weint Ihr?
MIRANDA. Um meinen Unwert, dass ich nicht darf bieten,
Was ich zu geben wünsche; noch viel minder,
Wonach ich tot mich sehnen werde, nehmen.
Doch das heißt Tändeln, und je mehr es sucht
Sich zu verbergen, um so mehr erscheint's
In seiner ganzen Macht. Fort, blöde Schlauheit!
Führ' du das Wort mir, schlichte, heil'ge Unschuld!
Ich bin Eu'r Weib, wenn Ihr mich haben wollt,
Sonst sterb' ich Eure Magd; Ihr könnt mir's weigern,
Gefährtin Euch zu sein, doch Dienerin
Will ich Euch sein: Ihr wollet oder nicht.

FERDINAND. My mistress, dearest,
    And I thus humble ever.
MIRANDA. My husband then?
FERDINAND. Ay, with a heart as willing
    As bondage e'er of freedom. Here's my hand.

MIRANDA. And mine, with my heart in't. And now farewell
    Till half an hour hence.

FERDINAND. A thousand, thousand!

Exeunt, Ferdinand and Miranda severally.

PROSPERO. So glad of this as they I cannot be,
    Who are surpris'd withal; but my rejoicing
    At nothing can be more. I'll to my book,
    For yet ere supper-time must I perform
    Much business appertaining. *Exit.*

Scene II

Enter Caliban, Stephano, and Trinculo.

STEPHANO. Tell not me. When the butt is out, we will drink water – not
    a drop before; therefore bear up and board 'em. Servant-monster, drink
    to me.
TRINCULO. Servant-monster? the folly of this island! They say there's but
    five upon this isle: we are three of them; if th' other two be brain'd like
    us, the state totters.
STEPHANO. Drink, servant-monster, when I bid thee. Thy eyes are al-
    most set in thy head.
TRINCULO. Where should they be set else? He were a brave monster
    indeed if they were set in his tail.
STEPHANO. My man-monster hath drown'd his tongue in sack. For my
    part, the sea cannot drown me; I swam, ere I could recover the shore, five
    and thirty leagues off and on. By this light, thou shalt be my lieutenant,
    monster, or my standard.

TRINCULO. Your lieutenant if you list, he's no standard.

STEPHANO. We'll not run, Monsieur Monster.
TRINCULO. Nor go neither; but you'll lie like dogs, and yet say nothing
    neither.
STEPHANO. Moon-calf, speak once in thy life, if thou beest a good
    moon-calf.

FERDINAND. Geliebte, Herrin, und auf immer ich
    So untertänig!
MIRANDA. Mein Gatte denn?
FERDINAND. Ja, mit so will'gem Herzen,
    Als Dienstbarkeit sich je zur Freiheit wandte.
    Hier habt Ihr meine Hand!
MIRANDA. Und Ihr die meine,
    Mit meinem Herzen drin; und nun lebt wohl
    Auf eine halbe Stunde!
FERDINAND. Tausend, tausendmal!

Ab, Ferdinand und Miranda separat.

PROSPERO. So froh wie sie kann ich nicht drüber sein,
    Die alles überrascht; doch größre Freude
    Gewährt mir nichts.
    Ich will zu meinem Buch,
    Denn vor der Abendmahlzeit hab' ich noch
    Viel Nöt'ges zu verrichten. *Ab.*

Zweite Szene

Caliban, Stephano und Trinculo kommen.

STEPHANO. Sagt mir da nicht von! Wenn das Fass leer ist, wollen wir
    Wasser trinken. Vorher keinen Tropfen! Also haltet Euch frisch und
    stecht sie an. Diener-Ungeheuer, tu' mir Bescheid!
TRINCULO. Diener-Ungeheuer? Ein tolles Stück von Insel! Sie sagen, es
    wären nur fünfe auf dieser Insel: wir sind drei davon; wenn die andern
    beiden so gehirnt sind wie wir, so wackelt der Staat.
STEPHANO. Trink, Diener-Ungeheuer, wenn ich dir's heiße. Die Augen
    stecken dir fast ganz im Kopfe drinnen.
TRINCULO. Wo sollten sie sonst stecken? Er wäre wahrlich ein prächtiges
    Ungeheuer, wenn sie ihm im Schweife steckten.
STEPHANO. Mein Kerl-Ungeheuer hat seine Zunge in Sekt ersäuft. Was
    mich betrifft, mich kann das Meer nicht ersäufen. Ich schwamm, eh' ich
    wieder ans Land kommen konnte, fünfunddreißig Meilen, ab und zu:
    beim Element! – Du sollst mein Leutnant sein, Ungeheuer, oder mein
    Fähnrich.
TRINCULO. Euer Leutnant, wenn's Euch beliebt: er kann die Fahne nicht
    halten.
STEPHANO. Wir werden nicht laufen, Musje Ungeheuer.
TRINCULO. Gehn auch nicht; Ihr werdet liegen wie Hunde und den
    Mund nicht auftun.
STEPHANO. Mondkalb, sprich einmal in deinem Leben, wenn du ein
    gutes Mondkalb bist.

CALIBAN. How does thy honor? Let me lick thy shoe. I'll not serve him,
he is not valiant.
TRINCULO. Thou liest, most ignorant monster, I am in case to justle a
constable. Why, thou debosh'd fish thou, was there ever man a coward
that hath drunk so much sack as I to-day? Wilt thou tell a monstrous lie,
being but half a fish and half a monster?

CALIBAN. Lo, how he mocks me! Wilt thou let him, my lord?

TRINCULO. »Lord,« quoth he? That a monster should be such a natural!

CALIBAN. Lo, lo again. Bite him to death, I prithee.
STEPHANO. Trinculo, keep a good tongue in your head. If you prove a
mutineer – the next tree! The poor monster's my subject, and he shall
not suffer indignity.
CALIBAN. I thank my noble lord. Wilt thou be pleas'd to hearken once
again to the suit I made to thee?
STEPHANO. Marry, will I; kneel, and repeat it. I will stand, and so shall
Trinculo.

Enter Ariel, invisible.

CALIBAN. As I told thee before,
I am subject to a tyrant,
A sorcerer, that by his cunning hath
Cheated me of the island.
ARIEL. Thou liest.
CALIBAN. Thou liest, thou jesting monkey thou!
I would my valiant master would destroy thee.
I do not lie.
STEPHANO. Trinculo, if you trouble him any more in 's tale, by this hand,
I will supplant some of your teeth.
TRINCULO. Why, I said nothing.
STEPHANO. Mum then, and no more. – Proceed.
CALIBAN. I say by sorcery he got this isle;
From me he got it. If thy greatness will
Revenge it on him – for I know thou dar'st,
But this thing dare not –
STEPHANO. That's most certain.
CALIBAN. Thou shalt be lord of it, and I'll serve thee.
STEPHANO. How now shall this be compass'd? Canst thou bring me to
the party?
CALIBAN. Yea, yea, my lord. I'll yield him thee asleep,
Where thou mayst knock a nail into his head.
ARIEL. Thou liest, thou canst not.
CALIBAN. What a pied ninny's this! Thou scurvy patch!
I do beseech thy greatness, give him blows,

CALIBAN. Wie geht's deiner Gnaden? Lass mich deine Schuh' lecken. Ihm will ich nicht dienen, er ist nicht herzhaft.

TRINCULO. Du lügst, unwissendes Ungeheuer. Ich bin imstande, einem Bettelvogt die Spitze zu bieten. Ei, du liederlicher Fisch du, war jemals einer eine Memme, der so viel Sekt getrunken hat als ich heute? Willst du eine ungeheure Lüge sagen, da du nur halb ein Fisch und halb ein Ungeheuer bist?

CALIBAN. Sieh, wie er mich zum besten hat: willst du das zugeben, mein Fürst?

TRINCULO. Fürst, sagt er? – Dass ein Ungeheuer solch ein Einfaltspinsel sein kann!

CALIBAN. Sieh, sieh! schon wieder! Bitte, beiß' ihn tot!

STEPHANO. Trinculo, kein loses Maul! Wenn Ihr aufrührisch werdet, soll der nächste Baum – das arme Ungeheuer ist mein Untertan, und ihm soll nicht unwürdig begegnet werden.

CALIBAN. Ich danke meinem gnädigen Herrn. Willst du geruhn, nochmals auf mein Gesuch zu hören, das ich dir vorbrachte?

STEPHANO. Ei freilich will ich: knie' und wiederhol' es! Ich will stehn, und das soll Trinculo auch.

Ariel kommt, unsichtbar.

CALIBAN. Wie ich dir vorher sagte,
Ich bin einem Tyrannen untertan,
Einem Zauberer, der mich durch seine List
Um die Insel betrogen hat.

ARIEL. Du lügst.

CALIBAN. Du lügst, du possenhafter Affe, du!
Dass dich mein tapfrer Herr verderben möchte!
Ich lüge nicht.

STEPHANO. Trinculo, wenn Ihr ihn in seiner Erzählung noch irgend stört, bei dieser Faust! ich schlag' Euch ein paar Zähne ein.

TRINCULO. Nun, ich sagte ja nichts.

STEPHANO. St also, und nichts weiter! – Fahre fort!

CALIBAN. Durch Zauberei gewann er diese Insel,
Gewann von mir sie. Wenn nun deine Hoheit
Ihn strafen will – ich weiß, du hast das Herz,
Doch dies Ding hier hat keins –

STEPHANO. Das ist gewiss.

CALIBAN. So sollst du Herr drauf sein, ich will dir dienen.

STEPHANO. Aber wie kommen wir damit zustande? Kannst du mir zu dem Handel Anweisung geben?

CALIBAN. Ja, ja, mein Fürst! Ich liefr' ihn dir im Schlaf,
Wo du ihm seinen Kopf durchnageln kannst.

ARIEL. Du lügst, du kannst nicht.

CALIBAN. Der scheckige Hanswurst! Du lump'ger Narr! –
Ich bitte deine Hoheit, gib ihm Schläge,

And take his bottle from him. When that's gone,
He shall drink nought but brine, for I'll not show him
Where the quick freshes are.
STEPHANO. Trinculo, run into no further danger; interrupt the monster
one word further, and by this hand, I'll turn my mercy out o' doors, and
make a stock-fish of thee.
TRINCULO. Why, what did I? I did nothing. I'll go farther off.

STEPHANO. Didst thou not say he lied?
ARIEL. Thou liest.
STEPHANO. Do I so? Take thou that. *Beats Trinculo.* As you like this, give
me the lie another time.
TRINCULO. I did not give the lie. Out o' your wits, and hearing too? A
pox o' your bottle! this can sack and drinking do. A murrain on your
monster, and the devil take your fingers!

CALIBAN. Ha, ha, ha!
STEPHANO. Now forward with your tale. – Prithee stand further off.
CALIBAN. Beat him enough. After a little time
I'll beat him too.
STEPHANO. Stand farther. – Come, proceed.
CALIBAN. Why, as I told thee, 'tis a custom with him
I' th' afternoon to sleep. There thou mayst brain him,
Having first seiz'd his books; or with a log
Batter his skull, or paunch him with a stake,
Or cut his wezand with thy knife. Remember
First to possess his books; for without them
He's but a sot, as I am; nor hath not
One spirit to command: they all do hate him
As rootedly as I. Burn but his books.
He has brave utensils (for so he calls them)
Which when he has a house, he'll deck withal.
And that most deeply to consider is
The beauty of his daughter. He himself
Calls her a nonpareil. I never saw a woman
But only Sycorax my dam and she;
But she as far surpasseth Sycorax
As great'st does least.

STEPHANO. Is it so brave a lass?
CALIBAN. Ay, lord, she will become thy bed, I warrant,
And bring thee forth brave brood.

Und nimm ihm seine Flasche; ist die fort,
So mag er Lake trinken, denn ich zeig' ihm
Die frischen Quellen nicht.
STEPHANO. Trinculo, stürze dich in keine weitere Gefahr: Unterbrich das
Ungeheuer noch mit einem Worte, und, bei dieser Faust, ich gebe meiner
Barmherzigkeit den Abschied und mache einen Stockfisch aus dir.
TRINCULO. Wie? Was hab' ich getan? Ich habe nichts getan, ich will
weiter weggehn.
STEPHANO. Sagtest du nicht, er löge?
ARIEL. Du lügst.
STEPHANO. Lüg' ich? Da hast du was. *Schlägt Trinculo.* Wenn du das gern
hast, straf mich ein andermal Lügen.
TRINCULO. Ich strafte Euch nicht Lügen. – Seid Ihr um Euern Verstand
gekommen, und ums Gehör auch? Zum Henker Eure Flasche! So weit
kann Sekt und Trinken einen bringen. – Dass die Pestilenz Euer Unge-
heuer, und hol' der Teufel Eure Finger!
CALIBAN. Ha ha ha!
STEPHANO. Nun weiter in der Erzählung. – Ich bitte dich, steh beiseite.
CALIBAN. Schlag' ihn nur tüchtig! Nach 'nem kleinen Weilchen
Schlag' ich ihn auch.
STEPHANO. Weiter weg! – Komm, fahre fort!
CALIBAN. Nun, wie ich sagte, 's ist bei ihm die Sitte,
Des Nachmittags zu ruhn; du kannst ihn würgen,
Hast du erst seine Bücher: mit 'nem Klotz
Den Schädel ihm zerschlagen, oder ihn
Mit einem Pfahl ausweiden, oder auch
Mit deinem Messer ihm die Kehl' abschneiden.
Denk' dran, dich erst der Bücher zu bemeistern,
Denn ohne sie ist er nur so ein Dummkopf,
Wie ich bin, und es steht kein einz'ger Geist
Ihm zu Gebot. Sie hassen alle ihn
So eingefleischt wie ich. Verbrenn' ihm nur
Die Bücher! Er hat schön Gerät (so nennt er's).
Sein Haus, wenn er eins kriegt, damit zu putzen.
Und was vor allem zu betrachten, ist
Die Schönheit seiner Tochter; nennt er selbst
Sie ohnegleichen doch. Ich sah noch nie ein Weib
Als meine Mutter Sycorax und sie:
Doch sie ist so weit über Sycorax,
Wie 's Größte übers Kleinste.
STEPHANO. Ist es so 'ne schmucke Dirne?
CALIBAN. Ja, Herr, sie wird wohl anstehn deinem Bett,
Das schwör' ich dir, und wackre Brut dir bringen.

STEPHANO. Monster, I will kill this man. His daughter and I will be king
    and queen – 'save our Graces! and Trinculo and thyself shall be viceroys.
    Dost thou like the plot, Trinculo?

TRINCULO. Excellent.
STEPHANO. Give me thy hand. I am sorry I beat thee; but while thou
    liv'st keep a good tongue in thy head.
CALIBAN. Within this half hour will he be asleep.
    Wilt thou destroy him then?
STEPHANO. Ay, on mine honor.
ARIEL. This will I tell my master.
CALIBAN. Thou mak'st me merry; I am full of pleasure,
    Let us be jocund. Will you troll the catch
    You taught me but while-ere?
STEPHANO. At thy request, monster, I will do reason, any reason. Come
    on, Trinculo, let us sing.

Sings.

  »Flout 'em and scout 'em,
  And scout 'em and flout 'em!
   Thought is free.«
CALIBAN. That's not the tune.

Ariel plays the tune on a tabor and pipe.

STEPHANO. What is this same?
TRINCULO. This is the tune of our catch, play'd by the picture of Nobody.

STEPHANO. If thou beest a man, show thyself in thy likeness. If thou
    beest a devil, take't as thou list.
TRINCULO. O, forgive me my sins!
STEPHANO. He that dies pays all debts. I defy thee. Mercy upon us!

CALIBAN. Art thou afeard?
STEPHANO. No, monster, not I.
CALIBAN. Be not afeard, the isle is full of noises,
    Sounds, and sweet airs, that give delight and hurt not.
    Sometimes a thousand twangling instruments
    Will hum about mine ears; and sometime voices,
    That if I then had wak'd after long sleep,
    Will make me sleep again, and then in dreaming,
    The clouds methought would open, and show riches
    Ready to drop upon me, that when I wak'd
    I cried to dream again.

STEPHANO. Ungeheuer, ich will den Mann umbringen; seine Tochter
und ich, wir wollen König und Königin sein – es lebe unsre Hoheit!, und
Trinculo und du, ihr sollt Vizekönige werden. – Gefällt dir der Handel,
Trinculo?
TRINCULO. Vortrefflich!
STEPHANO. Gib mir deine Hand! Es tut mir leid, dass ich dich schlug:
aber hüte dich dein Lebelang vor losen Reden!
CALIBAN. In einer halben Stund' ist er im Schlaf:
Willst du ihn dann vertilgen?
STEPHANO. Ja, auf meine Ehre!
ARIEL. Dies meld' ich meinem Herrn.
CALIBAN. Du machst mich lustig, ich bin voller Freude:
So lasst uns jubeln! Wollt Ihr's Liedlein trällern,
Das Ihr mich erst gelehrt?
STEPHANO. Auf dein Begehren, Ungeheuer, will ich mich dazu ver-
stehn, mich zu allem verstehn. Wohlan, Trinculo, lass uns singen!

Singt.

    Neckt sie und zeckt sie,
      und zeckt sie und neckt sie!
         Gedanken sind frei!
CALIBAN. Das ist die Weise nicht.

Ariel spielt die Melodie mit Trommel und Pfeife.

STEPHANO. Was bedeutet das?
TRINCULO. Es ist die Weise unsers Liedes, vom Herrn Niemand aufge-
spielt.
STEPHANO. Wo du ein Mensch bist, zeige dich in deiner wahren Gestalt;
bist du ein Teufel, so tu', was du willst!
TRINCULO. O vergib mir meine Sünden!
STEPHANO. Wer da stirbt, zahlt alle Schulden. Ich trotze dir. – Gott sei
uns gnädig!
CALIBAN. Bist du in Angst?
STEPHANO. Nein, Ungeheuer, das nicht.
CALIBAN. Sei nicht in Angst! Die Insel ist voll Lärm,
Voll Tön' und süßer Lieder, die ergötzen
Und niemand Schaden tun. Mir klimpern manchmal
Viel tausend helle Instrument' ums Ohr,
Und manchmal Stimmen, die mich, wenn ich auch
Nach langem Schlaf erst eben aufgewacht,
Zum Schlafen wieder bringen: dann im Traume
War mir, als täten sich die Wolken auf
Und zeigten Schätze, die auf mich herab
Sich schütten wollten, dass ich beim Erwachen
Aufs neu' zu träumen heulte.

STEPHANO. This will prove a brave kingdom to me, where I shall have
    my music for nothing.
CALIBAN. When Prospero is destroy'd.
STEPHANO. That shall be by and by. I remember the story.

TRINCULO. The sound is going away. Let's follow it, and after do our
    work.
STEPHANO. Lead, monster, we'll follow. I would I could see this taborer;
    he lays it on.
TRINCULO. Wilt come? I'll follow Stephano.

Exeunt.

Scene III

Enter Alonso, Sebastian, Antonio, Gonzalo, Adrian, Francisco, etc.

GONZALO. By'r lakin, I can go no further, sir,
    My old bones aches. Here's a maze trod indeed
    Through forth-rights and meanders! By your patience,
    I needs must rest me.

ALONSO. Old lord, I cannot blame thee,
    Who am myself attach'd with weariness
    To th' dulling of my spirits. Sit down, and rest.
    Even here I will put off my hope, and keep it
    No longer for my flatterer. He is drown'd
    Whom thus we stray to find, and the sea mocks
    Our frustrate search on land. Well, let him go.

ANTONIO *aside to Sebastian.*
    I am right glad that he's so out of hope.
    Do not for one repulse forgo the purpose
    That you resolv'd t' effect.
SEBASTIAN *aside to Antonio.* The next advantage
    Will we take throughly.
ANTONIO *aside to Sebastian.* Let it be to-night,
    For now they are oppress'd with travail, they
    Will not, nor cannot, use such vigilance
    As when they are fresh.
SEBASTIAN *aside to Antonio.* I say to-night. No more.

Solemn and strange music; and Prosper on the top, invisible.

ALONSO. What harmony is this? My good friends, hark!

STEPHANO. Dies wird mir ein tüchtiges Königreich werden, wo ich mei-
ne Musik umsonst habe.
CALIBAN. Wenn Prospero vertilgt ist.
STEPHANO. Das soll bald geschehn: ich habe die Geschichte noch im
Kopf.
TRINCULO. Der Klang ist im Abzuge. Lasst uns ihm folgen und dann
unser Geschäft verrichten!
STEPHANO. Geh voran, Ungeheuer, wir wollen folgen. – Ich wollte, ich
könnte diesen Trommelschläger sehn; er hält sich gut.
TRINCULO. Willst kommen? Ich folge, Stephano.

Alle ab.

Dritte Szene

Alonso, Sebastian, Antonio, Gonzalo, Adrian, Francisco und andre.

GONZALO. Bei unsrer Frauen, Herr, ich kann nicht weiter.
    Die alten Knochen schmerzen mir; das heiß‘ ich
    Ein Labyrinth durchwandern, grade aus
    Und in geschlungnen Wegen! Mit Erlaubnis,
    Ich muss notwendig ausruhn.
ALONSO. Alter Herr,
    Ich kann dich drum nicht tadeln, da ich selbst
    Von Müdigkeit ergriffen bin, die ganz
    Die Sinne mir betäubt: setz‘ dich und ruh‘!
    Hier tu‘ ich mich der Hoffnung ab und halte
    Nicht länger sie als meine Schmeichlerin.
    Er ist ertrunken, den zu finden so
    Wir irre gehn, und des vergebnen Suchens
    Zu Lande lacht die See. Wohl, fahr‘ er hin!
ANTONIO *beiseite zu Sebastian.*
    Mich freut‘s, dass er so ohne Hoffnung ist.
    Gebt eines Fehlstreichs wegen nicht den Anschlag,
    Den Ihr beschlossen, auf!
SEBASTIAN *beiseite zu Antonio.* Den nächsten Vorteil
    Lasst ja uns recht ersehn!
ANTONIO *beiseite zu Sebastian.* Es sei zu Nacht.
    Denn nun, bedrückt von der Ermüdung, werden
    Und können sie sich nicht so wachsam halten
    Als wie bei frischer Kraft.
SEBASTIAN *beiseite zu Antonio.* Zu Nacht, sag‘ ich: nichts weiter!

Feierliche und seltsame Musik, und Prospero in der Höhe, unsichtbar.

ALONSO. Welch eine Harmonie? Horcht, gute Freunde!

GONZALO. Marvellous sweet music!

Enter several strange Shapes, bringing in a banket; and dance about it with gentle actions of salutations; and inviting the King, etc., to eat, they depart.

ALONSO. Give us kind keepers, heavens! what were these?
SEBASTIAN. A living drollery. Now I will believe
    That there are unicorns; that in Arabia
    There is one tree, the phoenix' throne, one phoenix
    At this hour reigning there.
ANTONIO. I'll believe both;
    And what does else want credit, come to me,
    And I'll be sworn 'tis true. Travellers ne'er did lie,
    Though fools at home condemn 'em.
GONZALO. If in Naples
    I should report this now, would they believe me?
    If I should say I saw such islanders
    (For, certes, these are people of the island),
    Who though they are of monstrous shape, yet note
    Their manners are more gentle, kind, than of
    Our human generation you shall find
    Many, nay, almost any.
PROSPERO *aside*. Honest lord,
    Thou hast said well; for some of you there present
    Are worse than devils.
ALONSO. I cannot too much muse
    Such shapes, such gesture, and such sound expressing
    Although they want the use of tongue a kind
    Of excellent dumb discourse.
PROSPERO *aside*. Praise in departing.
FRANCISCO. They vanish'd strangely.
SEBASTIAN. No matter, since
    They have left their viands behind; for we have stomachs.
    Will't please you taste of what is here?
ALONSO. Not I.
GONZALO. Faith, sir, you need not fear. When we were boys,
    Who would believe that there were mountaineers,
    Dew-lapp'd, like bulls, whose throats had hanging at 'em
    Wallets of flesh? or that there were such men
    Whose heads stood in their breasts? which now we find
    Each putter-out of five for one will bring us
    Good warrant of.
ALONSO. I will stand to, and feed,
    Although my last, no matter, since I feel
    The best is past. Brother, my lord the Duke,
    Stand to, and do as we.

GONZALO. Wundersam liebliche Musik!

Verschiedne seltsame Gestalten kommen und bringen eine besetzte Tafel. Sie tanzen mit freundlichen Gebärden der Begrüßung um dieselbe herum, und indem sie den König und die übrigen einladen zu essen, verschwinden sie.

ALONSO. Verleih' uns gute Wirte, Gott! Was war das?
SEBASTIAN. Ein lebend Puppenspiel. Nun will ich glauben,
    Dass es Einhörner gibt, dass in Arabien
    Ein Baum des Phönix Thron ist und ein Phönix
    Zur Stunde dort regiert.
ANTONIO. Ich glaube beides;
    Und was man sonst bezweifelt, komme her,
    Ich schwöre drauf, 's ist wahr. Nie logen Reisende,
    Schilt gleich zu Haus der Tor sie.
GONZALO. Meldet' ich
    Dies nun in Napel, würden sie mir's glauben?
    Sagt' ich, dass ich Eiländer hier gesehen
    (Denn sicher sind dies Leute von der Insel),
    Die, ungeheu'r gestaltet, dennoch, seht,
    Von sanftern, mildern Sitten sind, als unter
    Dem menschlichen Geschlecht ihr viele, ja
    Kaum einen finden werdet.
PROSPERO *beiseite.* Wackrer Mann,
    Du hast wohl recht! Denn manche dort von euch
    Sind mehr als Teufel.
ALONSO. Ich kann nicht satt mich wundern:
    Gestalten solcher Art, Gebärde, Klang,
    Die, fehlt gleich der Gebrauch der Zunge, trefflich
    Ein Stumm Gespräch aufführen.
PROSPERO *beiseite.* Lobt beim Ausgang!
FRANCISCO. Sie schwanden seltsam.
SEBASTIAN. Tut nichts, da sie uns
    Die Mahlzeit ließen, denn wir haben Mägen. –
    Beliebt's zu kosten, was hier steht?
ALONSO. Mir nicht.
GONZALO. Herr, hegt nur keine Furcht. In unsrer Jugend,
    Wer glaubte wohl, es gebe Bergbewohner
    Mit Wammen so wie Stier', an deren Hals
    Ein Fleischsack hing? Es gebe Leute, denen
    Der Kopf im Busen säße? als wovon
    Jetzt jeder, der sein Schifflein lässt versichern,
    Uns gute Kundschaft bringt.
ALONSO. Ich gehe dran und esse,
    Wär's auch mein letztes. Mag es! fühl' ich doch,
    Das Beste sei vorüber. – Bruder, Herzog,
    Geht dran und tut wie wir!

ARIEL. You are three men of sin, whom Destiny,
    That hath to instrument this lower world
    And what is in't, the never-surfeited sea
    Hath caus'd to belch up you; and on this island
    Where man doth not inhabit – you 'mongst men
    Being most unfit to live. I have made you mad;
    And even with such-like valor men hang and drown
    Their proper selves.

Alonso, Sebastian, etc. draw their swords.

    You fools! I and my fellows
    Are ministers of Fate. The elements,
    Of whom your swords are temper'd, may as well
    Wound the loud winds, or with bemock'd-at stabs
    Kill the still-closing waters, as diminish
    One dowle that's in my plume. My fellow ministers
    Are like invulnerable. If you could hurt,
    Your swords are now too massy for your strengths,
    And will not be uplifted. But remember
    (For that's my business to you) that you three
    From Milan did supplant good Prospero,
    Expos'd unto the sea (which hath requit it)
    Him, and his innocent child; for which foul deed
    The pow'rs, delaying (not forgetting), have
    Incens'd the seas and shores – yea, all the creatures,
    Against your peace. Thee of thy son, Alonso,
    They have bereft; and do pronounce by me
    Ling'ring perdition (worse than any death
    Can be at once) shall step by step attend
    You and your ways, whose wraths to guard you from –
    Which here, in this most desolate isle, else falls
    Upon your heads – is nothing but heart's sorrow,
    And a clear life ensuing.

He vanishes in thunder; then, to soft music, enter the Shapes again, and dance, with mocks and mows, and carrying out the table.

PROSPERO. Bravely the figure of this harpy hast thou
    Perform'd, my Ariel; a grace it had, devouring.
    Of my instruction hast thou nothing bated
    In what thou hadst to say; so with good life,

Donner und Blitz. Ariel kommt in Gestalt einer Harpyie, schlägt mit seinen Flügeln auf die Tafel, und vermittelst einer zierlichen Erfindung verschwindet die Mahlzeit.

ARIEL. Ihr seid drei Sündenmänner, die das Schicksal
    (Das diese niedre Welt, und was darinnen,
    Als Werkzeug braucht) der nimmersatten See
    Geboten auszuspein; und an dies Eiland,
    Von Menschen unbewohnt, weil unter Menschen
    Zu leben ihr nicht taugt. Ich macht' euch toll,
    Und grad in solchem Mut ersäufen, hängen
    Sich Menschen selbst.

Alonso, Sebastian und die übrigen ziehn ihre Degen.

    Ihr Toren! ich und meine Brüder
    Sind Diener des Geschicks; die Elemente,
    Die eure Degen härten, könnten wohl
    So gut den lauten Wind verwunden, oder
    Die stets sich schließenden Gewässer töten
    Mit eitlen Streichen, als am Fittig mir
    Ein Fläumchen kränken. Meine Mitgesandten sind
    Gleich unverwundbar: könntet ihr auch schaden,
    Zu schwer sind jetzt für eure Kraft die Degen
    Und lassen sich nicht heben. Doch bedenkt
    (Denn das ist meine Botschaft), dass ihr drei
    Den guten Prospero verstießt von Mailand,
    Der See ihn preisgabt, – die es nun vergolten, –
    Ihn und sein harmlos Kind; für welche Untat
    Die Mächte, zögernd, nicht vergessend, jetzt
    Die See, den Strand, ja alle Kreaturen
    Empöret gegen euern Frieden. Dich,
    Alonso, haben sie des Sohns beraubt,
    Verkünden dir durch mich: ein schleichend Unheil,
    Viel schlimmer als ein Tod, der einmal trifft,
    Soll Schritt vor Schritt auf jedem Weg dir folgen.
    Um euch zu schirmen vor derselben Grimm,
    Der sonst in diesem gänzlich öden Eiland
    Aufs Haupt euch fällt, hilft nichts als Herzensleid
    Und reines Leben künftig.

Er verschwindet unter Donnern; dann kommen die Gestalten bei einer sanften Musik wieder, tanzen mit allerlei Fratzengesichtern und tragen die Tafel weg.

PROSPERO. Gar trefflich hast du der Harpyie Bildung
    Vollführt, mein Ariel; ein Anstand war's, verschlingend!
    Von meiner Vorschrift hast du nichts versäumt,
    Was du zu sagen hattest; und so haben

And observation strange, my meaner ministers
Their several kinds have done. My high charms work,
And these, mine enemies, are all knit up
In their distractions. They now are in my pow'r;
And in these fits I leave them, while I visit
Young Ferdinand, whom they suppose is drown'd,
And his and mine lov'd darling.

Exit above.

GONZALO. I' th' name of something holy, sir, why stand you
In this strange stare?
ALONSO. O, it is monstrous! monstrous!
Methought the billows spoke, and told me of it;
The winds did sing it to me, and the thunder,
That deep and dreadful organ-pipe, pronounc'd
The name of Prosper; it did base my trespass.
Therefore my son i' th' ooze is bedded; and
I'll seek him deeper than e'er plummet sounded,
And with him there lie mudded. *Exit.*
SEBASTIAN. But one fiend at a time,
I'll fight their legions o'er.
ANTONIO. I'll be thy second.

Exeunt Sebastian and Antonio.

GONZALO. All three of them are desperate: their great guilt
Like poison given to work a great time after
Now gins to bite the spirits. I do beseech you
That are of suppler joints follow them swiftly,
And hinder them from what this ecstasy
May now provoke them to.
ADRIAN. Follow, I pray you.

Exeunt omnes.

Mit guter Art und seltsamen Gebräuchen
Auch meine untern Diener jeglicher
Sein Amt gespielt. Mein hoher Zauber wirkt,
Und diese meine Feinde sind gebunden
In ihrem Wahnsinn; sie sind in meiner Hand.
Ich lass' in diesem Anfall sie und gehe
Zum jungen Ferdinand, den tot sie glauben,
Und sein- und meinem Liebling.

Er verschwindet.

GONZALO. In heil'ger Dinge Namen, Herr, was steht Ihr
So seltsam starrend?
ALONSO. Oh, es ist grässlich! grässlich!
Mir schien, die Wellen riefen mir es zu,
Die Winde sangen mir es, und der Donner,
Die tiefe grause Orgelpfeife, sprach
Den Namen Prospero, sie rollte meinen Frevel.
Drum liegt mein Sohn im Schlamm gebettet, und
Ich will ihn suchen, wo kein Senkblei forschte.
Und mit verschlämmt da liegen. *Ab.*
SEBASTIAN. Gebt mir nur einen Teufel auf einmal,
So fecht' ich ihre Legionen durch!
ANTONIO. Ich steh' dir bei.

Sebastian und Antonio ab.

GONZALO. Sie alle drei verzweifeln; ihre große Schuld,
Wie Gift, das lang' nachher erst wirken soll,
Beginnt sie jetzt zu nagen. Ich ersuch' euch,
Die ihr gelenker seid, folgt ihnen nach
Und hindert sie an dem, wozu der Wahnsinn
Sie etwa treiben könnte.
ADRIAN. Folgt, ich bitt' euch!

Alle ab.

Act IV
Scene I

Enter Prospero, Ferdinand, and Miranda.

PROSPERO. If I have too austerely punish'd you,
    Your compensation makes amends, for I
    Have given you here a third of mine own life,
    Or that for which I live; who once again
    I tender to thy hand. All thy vexations
    Were but my trials of thy love, and thou
    Hast strangely stood the test. Here, afore heaven,
    I ratify this my rich gift. O Ferdinand,
    Do not smile at me that I boast her off,
    For thou shalt find she will outstrip all praise
    And make it halt behind her.

FERDINAND. I do believe it
    Against an oracle.
PROSPERO. Then, as my gift, and thine own acquisition
    Worthily purchas'd, take my daughter. But
    If thou dost break her virgin-knot before
    All sanctimonious ceremonies may
    With full and holy rite be minist'red,
    No sweet aspersion shall the heavens let fall
    To make this contract grow; but barren hate,
    Sour-ey'd disdain, and discord shall bestrew
    The union of your bed with weeds so loathly
    That you shall hate it both. Therefore take heed,
    As Hymen's lamps shall light you.

FERDINAND. As I hope
    For quiet days, fair issue, and long life,
    With such love as 'tis now, the murkiest den,
    The most opportune place, the strong'st suggestion
    Our worser genius can, shall never melt
    Mine honor into lust, to take away
    The edge of that day's celebration,
    When I shall think or Phoebus' steeds are founder'd
    Or Night kept chain'd below.
PROSPERO. Fairly spoke.
    Sit then and talk with her, she is thine own.
    What, Ariel! my industrious servant, Ariel!

Enter Ariel.

Vierter Aufzug
Erste Szene

Prospero, Ferdinand und Miranda treten auf.

PROSPERO. Hab' ich zu strenge Buß' Euch auferlegt,
    So macht es die Vergeltung gut: ich gab
    Euch einen Faden meines eignen Lebens,
    Ja das, wofür ich lebe; noch einmal
    Biet' ich sie deiner Hand. All deine Plage
    War nur die Prüfung deiner Lieb', und du
    Hast deine Probe wunderbar bestanden.
    Hier vor des Himmels Angesicht bestät'ge
    Ich dies mein reich Geschenk. O Ferdinand!
    Lächl' über mich nicht, dass ich mit ihr prahle:
    Denn du wirst finden, dass sie allem Lob
    Zuvoreilt und ihr nach es hinken lässt.
FERDINAND. Ich glaub' es auch,
    Selbst gegen ein Orakel.
PROSPERO. Als Gabe dann und selbsterworbnes Gut,
    Würdig erkauft, nimm meine Tochter! Doch
    Zerreißt du ihr den jungfräulichen Gürtel,
    Bevor der heil'gen Feierlichkeiten jede
    Nach hehrem Brauch verwaltet werden kann,
    So wird der Himmel keinen Segenstau
    Auf dieses Bündnis sprengen: dürrer Haß,
    Scheeläugiger Verdruss und Zwist bestreut
    Das Bett, das euch vereint, mit eklem Unkraut,
    Dass ihr es beide hasst. Drum hütet euch,
    So Hymens Kerz' euch leuchten soll!
FERDINAND. So wahr
    Ich stille Tag', ein blühendes Geschlecht
    Und langes Leben hoff' in solcher Liebe
    Als jetzo: nicht die dämmerigste Höhle,
    Nicht der bequemste Platz, die stärkste Lockung
    So unser böser Genius vermag,
    Soll meine Ehre je in Wollust schmelzen,
    Um abzustumpfen jenes Tages Feier,
    Wann Phöbus' Zug gelähmt mir dünken wird,
    Die Nacht gefesselt drunten.
PROSPERO. Wohl gesprochen!
    Sitz' denn und rede mit ihr, sie ist dein. –
    He, Ariel, mein geflissner Diener Ariel!

Ariel kommt.

ARIEL. What would my potent master? here I am.
PROSPERO. Thou and thy meaner fellows your last service
    Did worthily perform; and I must use you
    In such another trick. Go bring the rabble
    (O'er whom I give thee pow'r) here to this place.
    Incite them to quick motion, for I must
    Bestow upon the eyes of this young couple
    Some vanity of mine art. It is my promise,
    And they expect it from me.
ARIEL. Presently?
PROSPERO. Ay, with a twink.
ARIEL. Before you can say »come« and »go,«
    And breathe twice, and cry »so, so,«
    Each one, tripping on his toe,
    Will be here with mop and mow.
    Do you love me, master? no?

PROSPERO. Dearly, my delicate Ariel. Do not approach
    Till thou dost hear me call.
ARIEL. Well; I conceive. *Exit.*
PROSPERO. Look thou be true; do not give dalliance
    Too much the rein. The strongest oaths are straw
    To th' fire i' th' blood. Be more abstenious,
    Or else good night your vow!
FERDINAND. I warrant you, sir,
    The white cold virgin snow upon my heart
    Abates the ardor of my liver.
PROSPERO. Well.
    Now come, my Ariel, bring a corollary,
    Rather than want a spirit. Appear, and pertly!
    No tongue! all eyes! Be silent.

Soft music. Enter Iris.

IRIS. Ceres, most bounteous lady, thy rich leas
    Of wheat, rye, barley, fetches, oats, and pease;
    Thy turfy mountains, where live nibbling sheep,
    And flat meads thatch'd with stover, them to keep;
    Thy banks with pioned and twilled brims,
    Which spungy April at thy hest betrims,
    To make cold nymphs chaste crowns; and thy broom-groves,
    Whose shadow the dismissed bachelor loves,
    Being lass-lorn; thy pole-clipt vineyard,
    And thy sea-marge, sterile and rocky-hard,
    Where thou thyself dost air – the Queen o' th' sky,
    Whose wat'ry arch and messenger am I,
    Bids thee leave these, and with her sovereign Grace,

ARIEL. Was will mein großer Meister? Ich bin da.
PROSPERO. Vollbracht hast du mit den geringern Brüdern
    Den letzten Dienst geziemend; und ich brauch' Euch
    Aufs neu' zu so 'nem Streich. Geh, bring' hierher
    Den Pöbel, über den ich Macht dir leihe.
    Lass sie behänd sich regen, denn ich muss
    Die Augen dieses jungen Paares weiden
    Mit Blendwerk meiner Kunst; ich hab's versprochen,
    Und sie erwarten es von mir.
ARIEL. Sogleich?
PROSPERO. Jawohl, in einem Wink.
ARIEL. Eh' du kannst sagen: komm und geh.
    Atem holst und rufst: he he,
    Mach' ich, wie ich geh' und steh',
    Dass hier jeder auf der Zeh'
    Sich mit Hokuspokus dreh'!
    Liebst du mich, mein Meister? – Ne.
PROSPERO. Herzlich, mein guter Ariel! Bleib' entfernt,
    Bis du mich rufen hörst.
ARIEL. Gut, ich verstehe. *Ab.*
PROSPERO. Sieh zu, dass du dein Wort hältst! Lass dem Tändeln
    Den Zügel nicht zu sehr: die stärksten Schwüre
    Sind Stroh dem Feu'r im Blut. Enthalt' dich mehr.
    Sonst: gute Nacht, Gelübd'!
FERDINAND. Herr, seid versichert,
    Der weiße, kalte, jungfräuliche Schnee
    An meiner Brust kühlt meines Blutes Hitze.
PROSPERO. Gut!
    Nun komm, mein Ariel! Bring' ein Übrig's lieber,
    Als dass ein Geist uns fehlt; erschein', und artig! –
    Kein Mund! Ganz Auge! Schweigt!

Sanfte Musik. Iris tritt auf.

IRIS. Ceres, du milde Frau! Dein reiches Feld
    Voll Weizen, Roggen, Haber, Gerst' und Spelt;
    Die Hügel, wo die Schaf' ihr Futter rauben
    Und Wiesen, wo sie ruhn, bedeckt von Schauben;
    Die Bäche mit betulptem, buntem Bord,
    Vom wäss'rigen April verzieret auf dein Wort,
    Zu keuscher Nymphen Kränzen; dein Gesträuch,
    Wo der verstoßne Jüngling, liebebleich,
    Sein Leid klagt; deine pfahlgestützten Reben;
    Die Küsten, die sich felsig dürr erheben,
    Wo du dich sonnst: des Himmels Königin,
    Der Wasserbogen ich und Botin bin,
    Heißt dich die alle lassen und, geladen

Here on this grass-plot, in this very place,
    To come and sport. Her peacocks fly amain.

Juno descends slowly in her car.

    Approach, rich Ceres, her to entertain.

Enter Ceres.

CERES. Hail, many-colored messenger, that ne'er
    Dost disobey the wife of Jupiter;
    Who with thy saffron wings upon my flow'rs
    Diffusest honey-drops, refreshing show'rs,
    And with each end of thy blue bow dost crown
    My bosky acres and my unshrubb'd down,
    Rich scarf to my proud earth – why hath thy Queen
    Summon'd me hither, to this short-grass'd green?

IRIS. A contract of true love to celebrate,
    And some donation freely to estate
    On the bless'd lovers.
CERES. Tell me, heavenly bow,
    If Venus or her son, as thou dost know,
    Do now attend the Queen? Since they did plot
    The means that dusky Dis my daughter got,
    Her and her blind boy's scandall'd company
    I have forsworn.
IRIS. Of her society
    Be not afraid. I met her Deity
    Cutting the clouds towards Paphos; and her son
    Dove-drawn with her. Here thought they to have done
    Some wanton charm upon this man and maid,
    Whose vows are, that no bed-right shall be paid
    Till Hymen's torch be lighted; but in vain,
    Mars's hot minion is return'd again;
    Her waspish-headed son has broke his arrows,
    Swears he will shoot no more, but play with sparrows,
    And be a boy right out.

Juno alights.

CERES. Highest Queen of state,
    Great Juno, comes, I know her by her gait.
JUNO. How does my bounteous sister? Go with me
    To bless this twain, that they may prosperous be,
    And honor'd in their issue.

They sing.

Auf diesen Rasenplatz, mit ihrer Gnaden
Ein Fest begehn. – Schon fliegt ihr Pfauenpaar:

Juno steigt langsam in ihrem Wagen ab.

Komm, reiche Ceres, stelle dich ihr dar!

Ceres tritt auf.

CERES. Heil dir, vielfärb'ge Botin, die du sorgst,
    Wie du der Gattin Jovis stets gehorchst;
    Die du von Safranschwingen süßen Tau
    Herab mir schüttest auf die Blumenau,
    Und krönst mit deinem blauen Bogen schön
    Die offnen Flächen und bebüschten Höh'n,
    Ein Gürtel meiner stolzen Erde! Sprich:
    Warum entbietet deine Herrin mich
    Auf diesen kurzbegrasten Plan durch dich?
IRIS. Ein Bündnis treuer Liebe hier zu feiern
    Und eine Gabe willig beizusteuern
    Zum Heil des Paares.
CERES. Sag mir, Himmelsbogen,
    Du weißt's ja, kommt auch Venus hergezogen
    Mit ihrem Sohn? Seit ihre List ersann,
    Wodurch der düstre Dis mein Kind gewann,
    Verschwor ich ihre samt des kleinen Blinden
    Verrufene Gesellschaft.
IRIS. Sie zu finden
    Sei sorglos: ihre Gottheit traf ich schon,
    Wie sie nach Paphos hin, mit ihrem Sohn,
    Die Wolken teilt in ihrem Taubenwagen.
    Sie dachten hier den Sieg davon zu tragen
    Durch üpp'gen Zauber über diesen Mann
    Und diese Jungfrau, so den Schwur getan,
    Nicht zu vollziehn des Bettes heil'ge Pflichten,
    Bis Hymens Fackel brennt. Allein mitnichten!
    Mars' heiße Buhle machte sich davon,
    Zerbrochen hat die Pfeil' ihr wilder Sohn:
    Der Trotzkopf schwört, er will nicht weiter zielen,
    Ganz Junge sein und nur mit Spatzen spielen.

Juno landet.

CERES. Da kommt der Juno höchste Majestät:
    Ich kenne sie, wie stolz einher sie geht.
JUNO. Wie geht es, güt'ge Schwester? Kommt herbei,
    Dies Paar zu segnen, dass es glücklich sei
    Und Ruhm erleb' an Kindern!

Sie singen.

JUNO.
>	Honor, riches, marriage-blessing,
>	Long continuance, and increasing,
>	Hourly joys be still upon you!
>	Juno sings her blessings on you.

CERES.
>	Earth's increase, foison plenty,
>	Barns and garners never empty;
>	Vines with clust'ring bunches growing,
>	Plants with goodly burthen bowing;
>	Spring come to you at the farthest
>	In the very end of harvest!
>	Scarcity and want shall shun you,
>	Ceres' blessing so is on you.

FERDINAND. This is a most majestic vision, and
>	Harmonious charmingly. May I be bold
>	To think these spirits?

PROSPERO. Spirits, which by mine art
>	I have from their confines call'd to enact
>	My present fancies.

FERDINAND. Let me live here ever;
>	So rare a wond'red father and a wise
>	Makes this place Paradise.

Juno and Ceres whisper, and send Iris on employment.

PROSPERO. Sweet now, silence!
>	Juno and Ceres whisper seriously;
>	There's something else to do. Hush and be mute,
>	Or else our spell is marr'd.

IRIS. You nymphs, call'd Naiades, of the windring brooks,
>	With your sedg'd crowns and ever-harmless looks,
>	Leave your crisp channels, and on this green land
>	Answer your summons; Juno does command.
>	Come, temperate nymphs, and help to celebrate
>	A contract of true love; be not too late.

Enter certain Nymphs.

>	You sunburn'd sicklemen, of August weary,
>	Come hither from the furrow and be merry.
>	Make holiday; your rye-straw hats put on,
>	And these fresh nymphs encounter every one
>	In country footing.

JUNO.
> Ehre, Reichtum, Eh'bescherung,
> Lange Dauer und Vermehrung!
> Stündlich werde Lust zu teil euch!
> Juno singt ihr hohes Heil euch.

CERES.
> Hüll' und Füll', Gedeihen immer,
> Scheun' und Boden ledig nimmer;
> Reben, hoch voll Trauben rankend;
> Pflanzen, von der Bürde wankend;
> Frühling werd' euch schon erneuert,
> Wann der Herbst kaum eingescheuert!
> Dürftigkeit und Mangel meid' euch!
> Ceres' Segen so geleit' euch!

FERDINAND. Dies ist ein majestätisch Schauspiel, und
> Harmonisch zum Bezaubern. Darf ich diese
> Für Geister halten?

PROSPERO. Geister, die mein Wissen
> Aus ihren Schranken rief, um vorzustellen,
> Was mir gefällt.

FERDINAND. Hier lasst mich immer leben:
> So wunderherrlich Vater und Gemahl
> Macht mir den Ort zum Paradies.

Juno und Ceres sprechen leise, und senden Iris auf eine Botschaft.

PROSPERO. Still, Lieber!
> Juno und Ceres flüstern ernstiglich:
> Es gibt noch was zu tun. St! und seid stumm,
> Sonst ist der Zauber hin. –

IRIS. Ihr Nymphen von den Bächen, die sich schlängeln,
> Mit mildem Blick, im Kranz von Binsenstengeln!
> Verlasst die krummen Betten: auf dem Plan
> Allhier erscheinet: Juno sagt's euch an.
> Auf, keusche Nymphen, helft uns einen Bund
> Der treuen Liebe feiern: kommt zur Stund!

Verschiedene Nymphen kommen.

> Ihr braunen Schnitter, müde vom August!
> Kommt aus den Furchen her zu einer Lust:
> Macht Feiertag, schirmt euch mit Sommerhüten,
> Den frischen Nymphen hier die Hand zu bieten
> Zum Erntetanz!

*Enter certain Reapers, properly habited: they join with the Nymphs in a grace-
ful dance, towards the end whereof Prospero starts suddenly, and speaks; after
which, to a strange, hollow, and confused noise, they heavily vanish.*

PROSPERO *aside*. I had forgot that foul conspiracy
    Of the beast Caliban and his confederates
    Against my life. The minute of their plot
    Is almost come.

To the Spirits.

    Well done, avoid; no more.
FERDINAND. This is strange. Your father's in some passion
    That works him strongly.
MIRANDA. Never till this day
    Saw I him touch'd with anger, so distemper'd.
PROSPERO. You do look, my son, in a mov'd sort,
    As if you were dismay'd; be cheerful, sir.
    Our revels now are ended. These our actors
    (As I foretold you) were all spirits, and
    Are melted into air, into thin air,
    And like the baseless fabric of this vision,
    The cloud-capp'd tow'rs, the gorgeous palaces,
    The solemn temples, the great globe itself,
    Yea, all which it inherit, shall dissolve,
    And like this insubstantial pageant faded
    Leave not a rack behind. We are such stuff
    As dreams are made on; and our little life
    Is rounded with a sleep. Sir, I am vex'd;
    Bear with my weakness, my old brain is troubled.
    Be not disturb'd with my infirmity.
    If you be pleas'd, retire into my cell,
    And there repose. A turn or two I'll walk
    To still my beating mind.
FERDINAND, MIRANDA. We wish your peace.
PROSPERO *to Ariel.*
    Come with a thought.

To Ferdinand and Miranda.

    I thank thee.

Exeunt Ferdinand and Miranda.

    Ariel! come.

Enter Ariel.

ARIEL. Thy thoughts I cleave to. What's thy pleasure?

Verschiedene Schnitter kommen, sauber gekleidet, die sich mit den Nymphen zu einem anmutigen Tanze vereinigen. Gegen das Ende desselben fährt Prospero plötzlich auf und spricht, worauf sie unter einem seltsamen, dumpfen und verworfnen Getöse langsam verschwinden.

PROSPERO *beiseite.* Vergessen hatt' ich ganz den schnöden Anschlag
    Des Viehes Caliban und seiner Mitverschwornen,
    Mich umzubringen; und der Ausführung
    Minute naht. –

Zu den Geistern.

    Schon gut! Brecht auf! Nichts mehr!
FERDINAND. Seltsam! Eu'r Vater ist in Leidenschaft,
    Die stark ihn angreift.
MIRANDA. Nie bis diesen Tag
    Sah ich ihn so von heft'gem Zorn bewegt.
PROSPERO. Mein Sohn, Ihr blickt ja auf verstörte Weise,
    Als wäret Ihr bestürzt: seid gutes Muts!
    Das Fest ist jetzt zu Ende; unsre Spieler,
    Wie ich Euch sagte, waren Geister, und
    Sind aufgelöst in Luft, in dünne Luft.
    Wie dieses Scheines lockrer Bau, so werden
    Die wolkenhohen Türme, die Paläste,
    Die hehren Tempel, selbst der große Ball,
    Ja, was daran nur Teil hat, untergehn
    Und, wie dies leere Schaugepräng' erblasst,
    Spurlos verschwinden. Wir sind solcher Zeug
    Wie der zu Träumen, und dies kleine Leben
    Umfasst ein Schlaf. – Ich bin gereizt, Herr: habt
    Geduld mit mir; mein alter Kopf ist schwindlicht.
    Seid wegen meiner Schwachheit nicht besorgt.
    Wenn's dir gefällt, begib dich in die Zelle
    Und ruh' da; ich will auf und ab hier gehn,
    Um mein Gemüt zu stillen.
FERDINAND UND MIRANDA. Findet Frieden!
PROSPERO *zu Ariel.*
    Komm wie ein Wind!

Zu Ferdinand und Miranda.

    Ich dank' dir.

Ferdinand und Miranda ab.

    Ariel, komm!

Ariel kommt.

ARIEL. An deinen Winken häng' ich. Was beliebt dir?

PROSPERO. Spirit,
  We must prepare to meet with Caliban.
ARIEL. Ay, my commander. When I presented Ceres,
  I thought to have told thee of it, but I fear'd
  Lest I might anger thee.
PROSPERO. Say again, where didst thou leave these varlots?
ARIEL. I told you, sir, they were red-hot with drinking,
  So full of valor that they smote the air
  For breathing in their faces; beat the ground
  For kissing of their feet; yet always bending
  Towards their project. Then I beat my tabor,
  At which like unback'd colts they prick'd their ears,
  Advanc'd their eyelids, lifted up their noses
  As they smelt music. So I charm'd their ears
  That calf-like they my lowing follow'd through
  Tooth'd briers, sharp furzes, pricking goss, and thorns,
  Which ent'red their frail shins. At last I left them
  I' th' filthy-mantled pool beyond your cell,
  There dancing up to th' chins, that the foul lake
  O'erstunk their feet.
PROSPERO. This was well done, my bird.
  Thy shape invisible retain thou still.
  The trumpery in my house, go bring it hither,
  For scale to catch these thieves.
ARIEL. I go, I go. *Exit.*
PROSPERO. A devil, a born devil, on whose nature
  Nurture can never stick; on whom my pains,
  Humanely taken, all, all lost, quite lost;
  And as with age his body uglier grows,
  So his mind cankers. I will plague them all,
  Even to roaring.

Enter Ariel, loaden with glistering apparel, etc.

  Come, hang them on this line.

Prospero and Ariel remain, invisible. Enter Caliban, Stephano, and Trinculo, all wet.

CALIBAN. Pray you tread softly, that the blind mole may not
  Hear a foot fall; we now are near his cell.

STEPHANO. Monster, your fairy, which you say is a harmless fairy, has
  done little better than play'd the Jack with us.
TRINCULO. Monster, I do smell all horse-piss, at which my nose is in
  great indignation.

PROSPERO. Geist,
  Wir müssen gegen Caliban uns rüsten.
ARIEL. Ja, mein Gebieter; als ich die Ceres spielte,
  Wollt' ich dir's sagen, doch ich war besorgt,
  Ich möchte dich erzürnen.
PROSPERO. Sag noch einmal, wo ließest du die Buben?
ARIEL. Ich sagt' Euch, Herr, sie glühten ganz vom Trinken,
  Voll Mutes, dass sie hieben in den Wind,
  Weil er sie angehaucht; den Boden schlugen,
  Der ihren Fuß geküsst; doch stets erpicht
  Auf ihren Plan. Da rührt' ich meine Trommel;
  Wie wilde Füllen spitzten sie das Ohr
  Und machten Augen, hoben ihre Nasen,
  Als röchen sie Musik. Ihr Ohr betört' ich so,
  Dass sie wie Kälber meinem Brüllen folgten
  Durch scharfe Disteln, Stechginst, Strauch und Dorn,
  Die ihre Beine ritzten; endlich ließ ich
  Im grünen Pfuhl sie, jenseits Eurer Zelle,
  Bis an den Hals drin watend, dass die Lache
  Die Füße überstank.
PROSPERO. Gut so, mein Vogel!
  Behalt' die unsichtbare Bildung noch!
  Den Trödelkram in meinem Hause, geh,
  Bring' ihn hierher, dies Diebsvolk anzukörnen!
ARIEL. Ich geh'! Ich geh'! *Ab.*
PROSPERO. Ein Teufel, ein geborner Teufel ist's,
  An dessen Art die Pflege nimmer haftet,
  An dem die Mühe, die ich menschlich nahm,
  Ganz, ganz verloren ist, durchaus verloren;
  Und wie sein Leib durchs Alter garst'ger wird,
  Verstockt sein Sinn sich. Alle will ich plagen,
  Bis zum Gebrüll.

Ariel kommt zurück mit glänzenden Kleidungsstücken.

  Komm, häng's an diese Schnur!

Prospero und Ariel bleiben, unsichtbar. Caliban, Stephano und Trinculo kommen ganz durchnässt.

CALIBAN. Ich bitt' euch, tretet sacht! Der blinde Maulwurf
  Hör' unsern Fuß nicht fallen; wir sind jetzt
  Der Zelle nah.
STEPHANO. Ungeheuer, dein Elfe, von dem du sagst, er sei ein harmloser
  Elfe, hat eben nichts Bessers getan, als uns zum Narren gehabt.
TRINCULO. Ungeheuer, ich rieche lauter Pferdeharn, worüber meine
  Nase höchlich entrüstet ist.

STEPHANO. So is mine. Do you hear, monster? If I should take a displeasure against you, look you –
TRINCULO. Thou wert but a lost monster.
CALIBAN. Good my lord, give me thy favor still.
    Be patient, for the prize I'll bring thee to
    Shall hoodwink this mischance; therefore speak softly,
    All's hush'd as midnight yet.
TRINCULO. Ay, but to lose our bottles in the pool –
STEPHANO. There is not only disgrace and dishonor in that, monster, but an infinite loss.
TRINCULO. That's more to me than my wetting; yet this is your harmless fairy, monster!
STEPHANO. I will fetch off my bottle, though I be o'er ears for my labor.

CALIBAN. Prithee, my king, be quiet. Seest thou here,
    This is the mouth o' th' cell. No noise, and enter.
    Do that good mischief which may make this island
    Thine own for ever, and I, thy Caliban,
    For aye thy foot-licker.
STEPHANO. Give me thy hand. I do begin to have bloody thoughts.
TRINCULO. O King Stephano! O peer! O worthy Stephano! look what a wardrobe here is for thee!
CALIBAN. Let it alone, thou fool, it is but trash.
TRINCULO. O, ho, monster! we know what belongs to a frippery. O King Stephano!
STEPHANO. Put off that gown, Trinculo. By this hand, I'll have that gown.
TRINCULO. Thy Grace shall have it.
CALIBAN. The dropsy drown this fool! what do you mean
    To dote thus on such luggage? Let't alone
    And do the murther first. If he awake,
    From toe to crown he'll fill our skins with pinches,
    Make us strange stuff.
STEPHANO. Be you quiet, monster. Mistress line, is not this my jerkin? Now is the jerkin under the line. Now, jerkin, you are like to lose your hair, and prove a bald jerkin.
TRINCULO. Do, do; we steal by line and level, and't like your Grace.

STEPHANO. I thank thee for that jest; here's a garment for't. Wit shall not go unrewarded while I am king of this country. ›Steal by line and level‹ is an excellent pass of pate; there's another garment for't.

TRINCULO. Monster, come put some lime upon your fingers, and away with the rest.

STEPHANO. Meine auch. Hörst du, Ungeheuer? Sollt' ich ein Missfallen
auf dich werfen, siehst du –
TRINCULO. Du wärst ein geliefertes Ungeheuer.
CALIBAN. Mein bester Fürst, bewahr' mir deine Gunst;
Sei ruhig, denn der Preis, den ich dir schaffe,
Verdunkelt diesen Unfall: drum sprich leise,
's ist alles still wie Nacht.
TRINCULO. Ja, aber unsre Flaschen in dem Pfuhl zu verlieren!
STEPHANO. Das ist nicht nur eine Schmach und Beschimpfung, Unge-
heuer, sondern ein unermesslicher Verlust.
TRINCULO. Daran liegt mir mehr als an meinem Nasswerden; und das ist
nun dein harmloser Elfe, Ungeheuer!
STEPHANO. Ich will meine Flasche herausholen, käm' ich auch für die
Mühe bis über die Ohren hinein.
CALIBAN. Bitt' dich, sei still, mein König! Siehst du hier
Der Zelle Mündung: ohne Lärm hinein,
Und tu' den guten Streich, wodurch dies Eiland
Auf immer dein, und ich dein Caliban,
Dein Füßelecker werde.
STEPHANO. Gib mir die Hand: ich fange an, blutige Gedanken zu haben.
TRINCULO. O König Stephano! O Herr! O würd'ger Stephano!
Sieh, welch eine Garderobe hier für dich ist!
CALIBAN. Lass es doch liegen, Narr; es ist nur Plunder.
TRINCULO. O ho, Ungeheuer! Wir wissen, was auf den Trödel gehört. –
O König Stephano!
STEPHANO. Nimm den Mantel herunter, Trinculo; bei meiner Faust! ich
will den Mantel!
TRINCULO. Deine Hoheit soll ihn haben.
CALIBAN. Die Wassersucht ersäuf den Narr'n! Was denkt ihr,
Vergafft zu sein in solche Lumpen? Lasst,
Und tut den Mord erst; wacht er auf, er zwickt
Vom Wirbel bis zum Zeh' die Haut uns voll,
Macht seltsam Zeug aus uns.
STEPHANO. Halt' dich ruhig, Ungeheuer! Madame Linie, ist nicht dies
mein Wams? Nun ist das Wams unter der Linie; nun, Wams, wird dir
wohl das Haar ausgehn, und du wirst ein kahles Wams werden.
TRINCULO. Nur zu! nur zu! Wir stehlen recht nach der Schnur, mit Eurer
Hoheit Erlaubnis.
STEPHANO. Ich danke dir für den Spaß, da hast einen Rock dafür. Witz
soll nicht unbelohnt bleiben, solang' ich König in diesem Lande bin.
»Nach der Schnur stehlen«, ist ein kapitaler Einfall. Da hast du noch
einen Rock dafür.
TRINCULO. Komm, Ungeheuer, schmiere deine Finger, und fort mit dem
Übrigen!

CALIBAN. I will have none on't. We shall lose our time,
  And all be turn'd to barnacles, or to apes
  With foreheads villainous low.
STEPHANO. Monster, lay-to your fingers. Help to bear this away where
  my hogshead of wine is, or I'll turn you out of my kingdom. Go to, carry
  this.
TRINCULO. And this.
STEPHANO. Ay, and this.

A noise of hunters heard. Enter divers Spirits in shape of dogs and hounds, hunting them about; Prospero and Ariel setting them on.

PROSPERO. Hey, Mountain, hey!
ARIEL. Silver! there it goes, Silver!
PROSPERO. Fury, Fury! there, Tyrant, there! hark, hark!

Caliban, Stephano, and Trinculo are driven out.

  Go, charge my goblins that they grind their joints
  With dry convulsions, shorten up their sinews
  With aged cramps, and more pinch-spotted make them
  Than pard or cat o' mountain.
ARIEL. Hark, they roar!
PROSPERO. Let them be hunted soundly. At this hour
  Lies at my mercy all mine enemies.
  Shortly shall all my labors end, and thou
  Shalt have the air at freedom. For a little
  Follow, and do me service.

Exeunt.

CALIBAN. Ich will's nicht: wir verlieren unsre Zeit
    Und werden all' in Baumgäns' oder Affen
    Mit schändlich kleiner Stirn verwandelt werden.
STEPHANO. Ungeheuer, tüchtig angepackt! Hilf mir dies hintragen, wo
    mein Oxhoft Wein ist, oder ich jage dich zu meinem Königreich hinaus.
    Frisch! trage dies!
TRINCULO. Dies auch.
STEPHANO. Ja, und dies auch.

*Ein Getöse von Jägern wird gehört. Es kommen mehr Geister in Gestalt von
Hunden, und jagen sie umher. Prospero und Ariel hetzen diese an.*

PROSPERO. Sasa, Waldmann, sasa!
ARIEL. Tiger! da läuft's, Tiger!
PROSPERO. Packani Packan! Da, Sultan, da! Fass! fass!

Caliban, Stephano und Trinculo werden hinausgetrieben.

    Geh, heiß' die Kobold' ihr Gebein zermalmen
    Mit starren Zuckungen, die Sehnen straff
    Zusammenkrampfen und sie fleck'ger zwicken
    Als wilde Katz' und Panther.
ARIEL. Horch, sie brüllen!
PROSPERO. Lass brav herum sie hetzen! Diese Stunde
    Gibt alle meine Feind' in meine Hand;
    In kurzem enden meine Müh'n, und du
    Sollst frei die Luft genießen: auf ein Weilchen
    Folg' noch und tu' mir Dienst!

Alle ab.

Act V
Scene I

Enter Prospero in his magic robes, and Ariel.

PROSPERO. Now does my project gather to a head:
  My charms crack not; my spirits obey; and Time
  Goes upright with his carriage. How's the day?

ARIEL. On the sixt hour, at which time, my lord,
  You said our work should cease.

PROSPERO. I did say so,
  When first I rais'd the tempest. Say, my spirit,
  How fares the King and 's followers?
ARIEL. Confin'd together
  In the same fashion as you gave in charge,
  Just as you left them; all prisoners, sir,
  In the line-grove which weather-fends your cell;
  They cannot boudge till your release. The King,
  His brother, and yours, abide all three distracted,
  And the remainder mourning over them,
  Brimful of sorrow and dismay; but chiefly
  Him that you term'd, sir, ›the good old Lord Gonzalo,‹
  His tears runs down his beard like winter's drops
  From eaves of reeds. Your charm so strongly works 'em
  That if you now beheld them, your affections
  Would become tender.

PROSPERO. Dost thou think so, spirit?
ARIEL. Mine would, sir, were I human.
PROSPERO. And mine shall.
  Hast thou, which art but air, a touch, a feeling
  Of their afflictions, and shall not myself,
  One of their kind, that relish all as sharply
  Passion as they, be kindlier mov'd than thou art?
  Though with their high wrongs I am strook to th' quick,
  Yet, with my nobler reason, 'gainst my fury
  Do I take part. The rarer action is
  In virtue than in vengeance. They being penitent,
  The sole drift of my purpose doth extend
  Not a frown further. Go, release them, Ariel.
  My charms I'll break, their senses I'll restore,
  And they shall be themselves.
 ARIEL. I'll fetch them, sir.

Fünfter Aufzug
Erste Szene

Prospero in seiner Zaubertracht und Ariel treten auf.

PROSPERO. Jetzt naht sich der Vollendung mein Entwurf,
  Mein Zauber reißt nicht, meine Geister folgen,
  Die Zeit geht aufrecht unter ihrer Last.
  Was ist's am Tag?
ARIEL. Die sechste Stunde, Herr,
  Um welche Zeit Ihr sagtet, dass das Werk
  Ein Ende nehmen solle.
PROSPERO. Ja, ich sagt' es,
  Als ich den Sturm erregte. Sag, mein Geist,
  Was macht der König jetzt und sein Gefolg'?
ARIEL. Gebannt zusammen auf dieselbe Weise,
  Wie Ihr mir auftrugt; ganz wie Ihr sie ließt;
  Gefangen alle, Herr, im Lindenwäldchen.
  Das Eure Zelle schirmt: sie können sich
  Nicht rippeln, bis Ihr sie erlöst. Der König,
  Sein Bruder, Eurer, alle drei im Wahnsinn.
  Die andern trauren um sie, übervoll
  Von Gram und Schreck; vor allen er, den Ihr
  »Den guten alten Herrn Gonzalo« nanntet.
  Die Tränen rinnen ihm am Bart hinab,
  Wie Wintertropfen an der Trauf' aus Rohr.
  Eu'r Zauber greift sie so gewaltig an,
  Dass, wenn Ihr jetzt sie sähet, Eu'r Gemüt
  Erweichte sich.
PROSPERO. Glaubst du das wirklich, Geist?
ARIEL. Meins würd' es, wär' ich Mensch.
PROSPERO. Auch meines soll's.
  Hast du, der Luft nur ist, Gefühl und Regung
  Von ihrer Not? und sollte nicht ich selbst,
  Ein Wesen ihrer Art, gleich scharf empfindend,
  Leidend wie sie, mich milder rühren lassen?
  Obschon ihr Frevel tief ins Herz mir drang,
  Doch nehm' ich gegen meine Wut Partei
  Mit meinem edlern Sinn: der Tugend Übung
  Ist höher als der Rache; da sie reuig sind,
  Erstreckt sich meines Anschlags ein'ger Zweck
  Kein Stirnerunzeln weiter: geh, befrei' sie!
  Ich will den Zauber brechen, ihre Sinne
  Herstellen, und sie sollen nun sie selbst sein.
ARIEL. Ich will sie holen, Herr.

Exit. Prospero traces a magic circle with his staff.

PROSPERO. Ye elves of hills, brooks, standing lakes, and groves,
    And ye that on the sands with printless foot
    Do chase the ebbing Neptune, and do fly him
    When he comes back; you demi-puppets that
    By moonshine do the green sour ringlets make,
    Whereof the ewe not bites; and you whose pastime
    Is to make midnight mushrumps, that rejoice
    To hear the solemn curfew: by whose aid
    (Weak masters though ye be) I have bedimm'd
    The noontide sun, call'd forth the mutinous winds,
    And 'twixt the green sea and the azur'd vault
    Set roaring war; to the dread rattling thunder
    Have I given fire, and rifted Jove's stout oak
    With his own bolt; the strong-bas'd promontory
    Have I made shake, and by the spurs pluck'd up
    The pine and cedar. Graves at my command
    Have wak'd their sleepers, op'd, and let 'em forth
    By my so potent art. But this rough magic
    I here abjure; and when I have requir'd
    Some heavenly music (which even now I do)
    To work mine end upon their senses that
    This airy charm is for, I'll break my staff,
    Bury it certain fadoms in the earth,
    And deeper than did ever plummet sound
    I'll drown my book.

Solemn music. Here enters Ariel before; then Alonso, with a frantic gesture, at-
tended by Gonzalo; Sebastian and Antonio in like manner, attended by Adrian
and Francisco. They all enter the circle which Prospero had made, and there
stand charm'd; which Prospero observing, speaks.

    A solemn air, and the best comforter
    To an unsettled fancy, cure thy brains,
    Now useless, boil'd within thy skull! There stand,
    For you are spell-stopp'd.
    Holy Gonzalo, honorable man,
    Mine eyes, ev'n sociable to the show of thine,
    Fall fellowly drops. The charm dissolves apace,
    And as the morning steals upon the night,
    Melting the darkness, so their rising senses
    Begin to chase the ignorant fumes that mantle
    Their clearer reason. O good Gonzalo,
    My true preserver, and a loyal sir
    To him thou follow'st! I will pay thy graces

Ab. Prospero zeichnet mit seinen Leuten einen magischen Kreis.

PROSPERO. Ihr Elfen von den Hügeln, Bächen, Hainen;
　Und ihr, die ihr am Strand, spurloses Fußes,
　Den ebbenden Neptunus jagt und flieht,
　Wann er zurückkehrt; halbe Zwerge, die ihr
　Bei Mondschein grüne saure Ringlein macht,
　Wovon das Schaf nicht frisst; die ihr zur Kurzweil
　Die nächt'gen Pilze macht; die ihr am Klang
　Der Abendglock' euch freut; mit deren Hilfe
　(Seid ihr gleich schwache Fäntchen) ich am Mittag
　Die Sonn' umhüllt, aufrühr'sche Wind' entboten,
　Die grüne See mit der azurnen Wölbung
　In lauten Kampf gesetzt, den furchtbar'n Donner
　Mit Feu'r bewehrt, und Jovis' Baum gespalten
　Mit seinem eignen Keil, des Vorgebirgs
　Grundfest' erschüttert, ausgerauft am Knorren
　Die Ficht' und Zeder; Grüft', auf mein Geheiß,
　Erweckten ihre Toten, sprangen auf
　Und ließen sie heraus, durch meiner Kunst
　Gewalt'gen Zwang: doch dieses grause Zaubern
　Schwör' ich hier ab; und hab' ich erst, wie jetzt
　Ich's tue, himmlische Musik gefordert,
　Zu wandeln ihre Sinne, wie die luft'ge
　Magie vermag: so brech' ich meinen Stab,
　Begrab' ihn manche Klafter in die Erde,
　Und tiefer, als ein Senkblei je geforscht,
　Will ich mein Buch ertränken.

*Feierliche Musik. Ariel kommt zurück; Alonso folgt ihm mit rasender Gebärde,
begleitet von Gonzalo; Sebastian und Antonio ebenso, von Adrian und Francisco begleitet: sie treten alle in den Kreis, den Prospero gezogen hat, und stehn
bezaubert da. Prospero bemerkt es und spricht.*

　Ein feierliches Lied, der beste Tröster
　Zur Heilung irrer Phantasie! – Dein Hirn,
　Jetzt nutzlos, kocht im Schädel dir: da steht!
　Denn ihr seid festgebannt. –
　Heil'ger Gonzalo! ehrenwerter Mann!
　Mein Auge lässt, befreundet mit dem Tun
　Des deinen, brüderliche Tropfen fallen.
　Allmählich löst sich die Bezaub'rung auf,
　Und wie die Nacht der Morgen überschleicht,
　Das Dunkel schmelzend, fangen ihre Sinnen
　Erwachend an, den blöden Dunst zu scheuchen,
　Der noch die hellere Vernunft umhüllt:
　O wackerer Gonzalo! mein Erretter,

Home both in word and deed. Most cruelly
Didst thou, Alonso, use me and my daughter;
Thy brother was a furtherer in the act.
Thou art pinch'd for't now, Sebastian. Flesh and blood,
You, brother mine, that entertain'd ambition,
Expell'd remorse and nature, whom, with Sebastian
(Whose inward pinches therefore are most strong),
Would here have kill'd your king, I do forgive thee,
Unnatural though thou art. – Their understanding
Begins to swell, and the approaching tide
Will shortly fill the reasonable shores
That now lie foul and muddy. Not one of them
That yet looks on me, or would know me! Ariel,
Fetch me the hat and rapier in my cell.

Exit Ariel, and returns immediately.

I will disease me, and myself present
As I was sometime Milan. Quickly, spirit,
Thou shalt ere long be free.

Ariel sings and helps to attire him.

ARIEL.
Where the bee sucks, there suck I,
In a cowslip's bell I lie;
There I couch when owls do cry.
On the bat's back I do fly
After summer merrily.
Merrily, merrily shall I live now,
Under the blossom that hangs on the bough.
PROSPERO. Why, that's my dainty Ariel! I shall miss thee,
But yet thou shalt have freedom. So, so, so.
To the King's ship, invisible as thou art;
There shalt thou find the mariners asleep
Under the hatches. The master and the boatswain
Being awake, enforce them to this place;
And presently, I prithee.
ARIEL. I drink the air before me, and return
Or ere your pulse twice beat. *Exit.*
GONZALO. All torment, trouble, wonder, and amazement
Inhabits here. Some heavenly power guide us
Out of this fearful country!
PROSPERO. Behold, sir King,
The wronged Duke of Milan, Prospero.
For more assurance that a living prince

Und redlicher Vasall dem, so du folgst!
Ich will dein Wohltun reichlich lohnen, beides
Mit Wort und Tat. – Höchst grausam gingst du um
Mit mir, Alonso, und mit meiner Tochter;
Dein Bruder war ein Förderer der Tat –
Das nagt dich nun, Sebastian! – Fleisch und Blut,
Mein Bruder du, der Ehrgeiz hegte, austrieb
Gewissen und Natur; der mit Sebastian
(Des inn're Pein deshalb die stärkste) hier
Den König wollte morden! Ich verzeih' dir,
Bist du schon unnatürlich. – Ihr Verstand
Beginnt zu schwellen, und die nah'nde Flut
Wird der Vernunft Gestad' in kurzem füllen,
Das daliegt, schwarz und schlammig. – Nicht einer drunter,
Der schon mich ansäh' oder kennte. – Ariel,
Hol' mir den Hut und Degen aus der Zelle.

Ariel ab und kehrt sofort wieder.

Auf dass ich mich entlarv' und stelle dar
Als Mailand, so wie vormals. – Hurtig, Geist,
Du wirst nun eh'stens frei..

Ariel singt und hilft den Prospero ankleiden.

ARIEL.
Wo die Bien', saug' ich mich ein,
Bette mich in Maiglöcklein,
Lausche da, wenn Eulen schrein,
Fliege mit der Schwalben Reih'n
Lustig hinterm Sommer drein.
Lustiglich, lustiglich leb' ich nun gleich
Unter den Blüten, die hängen am Zweig.
PROSPERO. Mein Liebling Ariel! Ja, du wirst mir fehlen,
Doch sollst du Freiheit haben. So, so, so!
Unsichtbar, wie du bist, zum Schiff des Königs,
Wo du das Seevolk schlafend finden wirst
Im Raum des Schiffs: den Schiffspatron und Bootsmann,
Sobald sie wach sind, nöt'ge sie hierher;
Und gleich, ich bitte dich.
ARIEL. Ich trink' im Flug die Luft und bin zurück,
Eh' zweimal Euer Puls schlägt. *Ab.*
GONZALO. Nur Qual, Verwirrung, Wunder und Entsetzen
Wohnt hier: führ' eine himmlische Gewalt uns
Aus diesem furchtbar'n Lande!
PROSPERO. Seht, Herr König,
Mailands gekränkten Herzog, Prospero:
Und zum Beweis, dass ein lebend'ger Fürst

Does now speak to thee, I embrace thy body,
And to thee and thy company I bid
A hearty welcome.
ALONSO. Whe'er thou beest he or no,
Or some enchanted trifle to abuse me
As late I have been, I not know. Thy pulse
Beats as of flesh and blood; and since I saw thee,
Th' affliction of my mind amends, with which
I fear a madness held me. This must crave
And if this be at all a most strange story.
Thy dukedom I resign, and do entreat
Thou pardon me my wrongs. But how should Prospero
Be living, and be here?
PROSPERO *to Gonzalo.* First, noble friend,
Let me embrace thine age, whose honor cannot
Be measur'd or confin'd.
GONZALO. Whether this be,
Or be not, I'll not swear.
PROSPERO. You do yet taste
Some subtleties o' th' isle, that will not let you
Believe things certain. Welcome, my friends all!

Aside to Sebastian and Antonio.

But you, my brace of lords, were I so minded,
I here could pluck his Highness' frown upon you
And justify you traitors. At this time
I will tell no tales.

SEBASTIAN *aside.* The devil speaks in him.
PROSPERO. No.
For you, most wicked sir, whom to call brother
Would even infect my mouth, I do forgive
Thy rankest fault – all of them; and require
My dukedom of thee, which perforce, I know
Thou must restore.
ALONSO. If thou beest Prospero,
Give us particulars of thy preservation,
How thou hast met us here, whom three hours since
Were wrack'd upon this shore; where I have lost
(How sharp the point of this remembrance is!)
My dear son Ferdinand.
PROSPERO. I am woe for't, sir.
ALONSO. Irreparable is the loss, and patience
Says, it is past her cure.

Jetzt mit dir spricht, umarm' ich deinen Körper
Und heiße dich und dein Gefolge herzlich
Willkommen hier.
ALONSO. Ob du es bist, ob nicht,
Ob ein bezaubert Spielwerk, mich zu täuschen,
Wie ich noch eben, weiß ich nicht: dein Puls
Schlägt wie von Fleisch und Blut; seit ich dich sah,
Genas die Seelenangst, womit ein Wahnsinn
Mich drückte, wie ich fürchte. Dies erfordert,
Wenn's wirklich ist, die seltsamste Geschichte.
Dein Herzogtum geb' ich zurück, und bitte,
Vergib mein Unrecht mir! – Doch wie kann Prospero
Am Leben sein und hier?
PROSPERO *zu Gonzalo*. Erst, edler Freund,
Lass mich dein Alter herzen, dessen Ehre
Nicht Maß noch Grenze kennt.
GONZALO. Ob dies so ist,
Ob nicht, will ich nicht schwören.
PROSPERO. Ihr erprobt
Kunststücke dieser Insel noch, die Euch
Nicht für gewiss die Dinge halten lassen.
Willkommen, meine Freunde!

Beiseite zu Antonio und Sebastian.

Aber ihr,
Mein Paar von Herren, wär' ich so gesinnt,
Ich könnte seiner Hoheit Zorn euch zuziehn
Und des Verrats euch zeihen: doch ich will
Nicht plaudern jetzt.
SEBASTIAN *beiseite*. Der Teufel spricht aus ihm.
PROSPERO. Nein. –
Euch, schlechter Herr, den Bruder nur zu nennen
Schon meinen Mund beflecken würd', erlass' ich
Den ärgsten Fehltritt; alle; und verlange
Mein Herzogtum von dir, das du, ich weiß,
Durchaus musst wiedergeben.
ALONSO. Bist du Prospero,
Meld' uns das Nähere von deiner Rettung;
Wie du uns trafst, die vor drei Stunden hier
Am Strand gescheitert, wo für mich verloren
(Wie scharf der Stachel der Erinn'rung ist!)
Mein Sohn! mein Ferdinand!
PROSPERO. Herr, ich beklag's.
ALONSO. Unheilbar ist der Schad', und die Geduld
Sagt, sie vermag hier nichts.

PROSPERO. I rather think
    You have not sought her help, of whose soft grace
    For the like loss I have her sovereign aid,
    And rest myself content.

ALONSO. You the like loss?
PROSPERO. As great to me as late, and supportable
    To make the dear loss, have I means much weaker
    Than you may call to comfort you; for I
    Have lost my daughter.
ALONSO. A daughter?
    O heavens, that they were living both in Naples,
    The King and Queen there! That they were, I wish
    Myself were mudded in that oozy bed
    Where my son lies. When did you lose your daughter?

PROSPERO. In this last tempest. I perceive these lords
    At this encounter do so much admire
    That they devour their reason, and scarce think
    Their eyes do offices of truth, their words
    Are natural breath; but howsoev'r you have
    Been justled from your senses, know for certain
    That I am Prospero, and that very duke
    Which was thrust forth of Milan, who most strangely
    Upon this shore where you were wrack'd was landed,
    To be the lord on't. No more yet of this,
    For 'tis a chronicle of day by day,
    Not a relation for a breakfast, nor
    Befitting this first meeting. Welcome, sir;
    This cell's my court. Here have I few attendants,
    And subjects none abroad. Pray you look in.
    My dukedom since you have given me again,
    I will requite you with as good a thing,
    At least bring forth a wonder, to content ye
    As much as me my dukedom.

Here Prospero discovers Ferdinand and Miranda playing at chess.

MIRANDA. Sweet lord, you play me false.
FERDINAND. No, my dearest love,
    I would not for the world.
MIRANDA. Yes, for a score of kingdoms you should wrangle,
    And I would call it fair play.

PROSPERO. Ich denke eher,
    Ihr suchtet ihre Hilfe nicht, durch deren
    Sanftmüt'ge Huld bei ähnlichem Verlust
    Ich ihres hohen Beistands teilhaft ward
    Und mich zufrieden gab.
ALONSO. Ihr ähnlichen Verlust?
PROSPERO. Gleich groß für mich, gleich neu; und ihn erträglich
    Zu finden, hab' ich doch weit schwächre Mittel,
    Als Ihr zum Trost herbei könnt rufen: ich
    Verlor ja meine Tochter.
ALONSO. Eine Tochter?
    O Himmel! wären sie doch beid' in Napel
    Am Leben, König dort und Königin!
    Wenn sie's nur wären, wünscht' ich selbst versenkt
    In jenes schlamm'ge Bett zu sein, wo jetzt
    Mein Sohn liegt. Wann verlort Ihr Eure Tochter?
PROSPERO. Im letzten Sturm. Ich merke, diese Herrn
    Sind ob dem Vorfall so verwundert, dass
    Sie ihren Witz verschlingen und kaum denken,
    Ihr Aug' bediene recht sie, ihre Worte
    Sei'n wahrer Odem; doch, wie sehr man euch
    Gedrängt aus euren Sinnen, wisst gewiss,
    Dass Prospero ich bin, derselbe Herzog,
    Von Mailand einst verstoßen; der höchst seltsam
    An diesem Strand, wo ihr gescheitert, ankam,
    Hier Herr zu sein. Nichts weiter noch hiervon!
    Denn eine Chronik ist's von Tag zu Tag,
    Nicht ein Bericht bei einem Frühstück, noch
    Dem ersten Wiedersehen angemessen.
    Willkommen, Herr! Die Zell' da ist mein Hof.
    Hier hab' ich nur ein klein Gefolg', und auswärts
    Nicht einen Untertan: seht doch hinein!
    Weil Ihr mein Herzogtum mir wiedergebt,
    Will ich's mit eben so was Gutem lohnen,
    Ein Wunder mind'stens auftun, dass Euch freue
    So sehr als mich mein Herzogtum.

*Der Eingang der Zelle öffnet sich, und man sieht Ferdinand und Miranda, die
Schach zusammen spielen.*

MIRANDA. Mein Prinz, Ihr spielt mir falsch.
FERDINAND. Mein teures Leben,
    Das tät' ich um die Welt nicht.
MIRANDA. Ja, um ein Dutzend Königreiche würdet
    Ihr hadern, und ich nennt' es ehrlich Spiel.

ALONSO. If this prove
    A vision of the island, one dear son
    Shall I twice lose.
SEBASTIAN. A most high miracle!
FERDINAND. Though the seas threaten, they are merciful;
    I have curs'd them without cause.

Kneels.

ALONSO. Now all the blessings
    Of a glad father compass thee about!
    Arise, and say how thou cam'st here.
MIRANDA. O wonder!
    How many goodly creatures are there here!
    How beauteous mankind is! O brave new world
    That has such people in't!
PROSPERO. 'Tis new to thee.
ALONSO. What is this maid with whom thou wast at play?
    Your eld'st acquaintance cannot be three hours.
    Is she the goddess that hath sever'd us,
    And brought us thus together?
FERDINAND. Sir, she is mortal;
    But by immortal Providence she's mine.
    I chose her when I could not ask my father
    For his advice, nor thought I had one. She
    Is daughter to this famous Duke of Milan,
    Of whom so often I have heard renown,
    But never saw before; of whom I have
    Receiv'd a second life; and second father
    This lady makes him to me.
ALONSO. I am hers.
    But O, how oddly will it sound that I
    Must ask my child forgiveness!
PROSPERO. There, sir, stop.
    Let us not burthen our remembrances with
    A heaviness that's gone.
GONZALO. I have inly wept,
    Or should have spoke ere this. Look down, you gods,
    And on this couple drop a blessed crown!
    For it is you that have chalk'd forth the way
    Which brought us hither.
ALONSO. I say amen, Gonzalo!
GONZALO. Was Milan thrust from Milan, that his issue
    Should become kings of Naples? O, rejoice
    Beyond a common joy, and set it down
    With gold on lasting pillars: in one voyage
    Did Claribel her husband find at Tunis,

ALONSO. Wenn dies nichts weiter ist als ein Gesicht
    Der Insel, werd' ich einen teuren Sohn
    Zweimal verlieren.
SEBASTIAN. Ein erstaunlich Wunder!
FERDINAND. Droht gleich die See, ist sie doch mild: ich habe
    Sie ohne Grund verflucht.

Er kniet nieder.

ALONSO. Nun, aller Segen
    Des frohen Vaters fasse rings dich ein!
    Steh auf und sag, wie kamst du her?
MIRANDA. O Wunder!
    Was gibt's für herrliche Geschöpfe hier!
    Wie schön der Mensch ist! Wackre neue Welt,
    Die solche Bürger trägt!
PROSPERO. Es ist dir neu.
ALONSO. Wer ist dies Mädchen da, mit dem du spieltest?
    Drei Stunden kaum kann die Bekanntschaft alt sein.
    Ist sie die Göttin, die uns erst getrennt,
    Und so zusammenbringt?
FERDINAND. Herr, sie ist sterblich,
    Doch durch unsterbliches Verhängnis mein.
    Ich wählte sie, als ich zu Rat den Vater
    Nicht konnte ziehn, noch glaubt', ich habe einen.
    Sie ist die Tochter dieses großen Herzogs
    Von Mailand, dessen Ruhm ich oft gehört,
    Doch nie zuvor ihn sah; von ihm empfing ich
    Ein zweites Leben, und zum zweiten Vater
    Macht ihn dies Fräulein mir.
ALONSO. Ich bin der ihre;
    Doch oh, wie seltsam klingt's, dass ich mein Kind
    Muss um Verzeihung bitten!
PROSPERO. Haltet, Herr:
    Lasst die Erinnerung uns nicht belasten
    Mit dem Verdrusse, der vorüber ist.
GONZALO. Ich habe innerlich geweint, sonst hätt' ich
    Schon längst gesprochen. Schaut herab, ihr Götter,
    Senkt eine Segenskron' auf dieses Paar!
    Denn ihr seid's, die den Weg uns vorgezeichnet,
    Der uns hierher gebracht.
ALONSO. Ich sage Amen!
GONZALO. Ward Mailand darum weggebannt von Mailand,
    Dass sein Geschlecht gelangt' auf Napels Thron?
    O freut mit seltner Freud' euch; grabt's mit Gold
    In ew'ge Pfeiler ein: auf einer Reise
    Fand Claribella den Gemahl in Tunis,

And Ferdinand, her brother, found a wife
Where he himself was lost; Prospero, his dukedom
In a poor isle; and all of us, ourselves,
When no man was his own.
ALONSO *to Ferdinand and Miranda.*
Give me your hands.
Let grief and sorrow still embrace his heart
That doth not wish you joy!
GONZALO. Be it so, amen!

Enter Ariel, with the Master and Boatswain amazedly following.

O, look, sir, look, sir, here is more of us.
I prophesied, if a gallows were on land,
This fellow could not drown. Now, blasphemy,
That swear'st grace o'erboard, not an oath on shore?
Hast thou no mouth by land? What is the news?

BOATSWAIN. The best news is, that we have safely found
Our king and company; the next, our ship –
Which, but three glasses since, we gave out split –
Is tight and yare, and bravely rigg'd as when
We first put out to sea.

ARIEL *aside to Prospero.* Sir, all this service
Have I done since I went.
PROSPERO *aside to Ariel.* My tricksy spirit!
ALONSO. These are not natural events, they strengthen
From strange to stranger. Say, how came you hither?
BOATSWAIN. If I did think, sir, I were well awake,
I'ld strive to tell you. We were dead of sleep,
And (how we know not) all clapp'd under hatches,
Where, but even now, with strange and several noises
Of roaring, shrieking, howling, jingling chains,
And moe diversity of sounds, all horrible,
We were awak'd; straightway, at liberty;
Where we, in all our trim, freshly beheld
Our royal, good, and gallant ship; our master
Cap'ring to eye her. On a trice, so please you,
Even in a dream, were we divided from them,
And were brought moping hither.

ARIEL *aside to Prospero.* Was't well done?
PROSPERO *aside to Ariel.* Bravely, my diligence. Thou shalt be free.

Und Ferdinand, ihr Bruder, fand ein Weib,
Wo man ihn selbst verloren; Prospero
Sein Herzogtum in einer armen Insel;
Wir all' uns selbst, da niemand sein war.
ALONSO *zu Ferdinand und Miranda.*
Gebt die Hände mir!
Umfasse Gram und Leid stets dessen Herz,
Der euch nicht Freude wünscht!
GONZALO. So sei es, Amen!

Ariel kommt mit dem Schiffspatron und Bootsmann, die ihm betäubt folgen.

O seht, Herr! seht, Herr! Hier sind unser mehr.
Ich prophezeite, gäb's am Lande Galgen,
So könnte der Geselle nicht ersaufen.
Nun, Lästerung, der du die Gottesfurcht
Vom Bord fluchst, keinen Schwur hier auf dem Trocknen?
Hast keinen Mund zu Land? Was gibt es Neues?
BOOTSMANN. Das beste Neue ist, dass wir den König
Und die Gesellschaft wohlbehalten sehn;
Das nächste: unser Schiff, das vor drei Stunden
Wir für gescheitert ansahn, ist so dicht,
So fest und brav getakelt, als da erst
In See wir stachen.
ARIEL *beiseite zu Prospero.* Herr, dies alles hab' ich
Besorgt, seitdem ich ging.
PROSPERO *beiseite zu Ariel.* Mein flinker Geist!
ALONSO. All dies geht nicht natürlich zu: von Wundern
Zu Wundern steigt es. – Sagt, wie kamt Ihr her?
BOOTSMANN. Herr, wenn ich dächte, ich wär' völlig wach,
Versucht' ich, Euch es kund zu tun. Wir lagen
In Totenschlaf und (wie, das weiß ich nicht)
All' in den Raum gepackt; da wurden wir
Durch wunderbar und mancherlei Getöse
Von Brüllen, Kreischen, Heulen, Kettenklirren
Und mehr Verschiedenheit von Lauten, alle grässlich,
Jetzt eben aufgeweckt; alsbald in Freiheit;
Wo wir in voller Pracht, gesund und frisch,
Sahn unser königliches, wackres Schiff,
Und der Patron sprang gaffend drum herum:
Als wir im Nu, mit Eurer Gunst, wie träumend
Von ihnen weggerissen und verdutzt
Hier wurden hergebracht.
ARIEL *beiseite zu Prospero.* Macht' ich es gut?
PROSPERO *beiseite zu Ariel.* Recht schön, mein kleiner Fleiß! Du wirst
auch frei.

ALONSO. This is as strange a maze as e'er men trod,
    And there is in this business more than nature
    Was ever conduct of. Some oracle
    Must rectify our knowledge.

PROSPERO. Sir, my liege,
    Do not infest your mind with beating on
    The strangeness of this business. At pick'd leisure,
    Which shall be shortly, single I'll resolve you
    (Which to you shall seem probable) of every
    These happen'd accidents; till when, be cheerful
    And think of each thing well.

Aside to Ariel.

    Come hither, spirit.
    Set Caliban and his companions free;
    Untie the spell.

Exit Ariel.

    How fares my gracious sir?
    There are yet missing of your company
    Some few odd lads that you remember not.

Enter Ariel, driving in Caliban, Stephano, and Trinculo in their stol'n apparel.

STEPHANO. Every man shift for all the rest, and let no man take care for
    himself; for all is but fortune. Coraggio, bully-monster, coraggio!

TRINCULO. If these be true spies which I wear in my head, here's a
    goodly sight.
CALIBAN. O Setebos, these be brave spirits indeed!
    How fine my master is! I am afraid
    He will chastise me.
SEBASTIAN. Ha, ha!
    What things are these, my Lord Antonio?
    Will money buy 'em?
ANTONIO. Very like; one of them
    Is a plain fish, and no doubt marketable.
PROSPERO. Mark but the badges of these men, my lords,
    Then say if they be true. This misshapen knave –
    His mother was a witch, and one so strong
    That could control the moon, make flows and ebbs,
    And deal in her command without her power.
    These three have robb'd me, and this demi-devil
    (For he's a bastard one) had plotted with them

ALONSO. Dies ist das wunderbarste Labyrinth,
Das je ein Mensch betrat; in diesem Handel
Ist mehr, als unter Leitung der Natur
Je vorging: ein Orakel muss darein
Uns Einsicht öffnen.
PROSPERO. Herr, mein Lehenshaupt,
Verstört nicht Eu'r Gemüt durch Grübeln über
Der Seltsamkeit des Handels; wenn wir Muße
Gesammelt, was in kurzem wird geschehn,
Will ich Euch Stück für Stück Erklärung geben,
Die Euch gegründet dünken soll, von jedem
Ereignis, das geschehn: so lang' seid fröhlich
Und denket gut von allem! –

Beiseite zu Ariel.

Geist, komm her!
Mach' Caliban und die Gesellen frei,
Lös' ihren Bann! –

Ariel ab.

Was macht mein gnäd'ger Herr?
Es fehlen vom Gefolg' Euch noch ein paar
Spaßhafte Bursche, die Ihr ganz vergesst.

*Ariel kommt zurück und treibt Caliban, Stephano und Trinculo in ihren ge-
stohlnen Kleidern vor sich her.*

STEPHANO. Jeder mache sich nur für alle übrigen zu schaffen, und keiner
sorge für sich selbst, denn alles ist nur Glück. – Courage, Blitzungeheuer,
Courage!
TRINCULO. Wenn dies wahrhafte Kundschafter sind, die ich im Kopfe
trage, so gibt es hier was Herrliches zu sehn.
CALIBAN. O Setebos, das sind mir wackre Geister!
Wie schön mein Meister ist! Ich fürchte mich,
Dass er mich zücht'gen wird.
SEBASTIAN. Ha, ha!
Was sind das da für Dinger, Prinz Antonio?
Sind sie für Geld zu Kauf?
ANTONIO. Doch wohl! Der eine
Ist völlig Fisch, und ohne Zweifel marktbar.
PROSPERO. Bemerkt nur dieser Leute Tracht, ihr Herrn,
Und sagt mir dann, ob sie wohl ehrlich sind.
Der missgeschaffne Schurke – seine Mutter
War eine Hex', und zwar so stark, dass sie
Den Mond in Zwang hielt, Flut und Ebbe machte
Und außer ihrem Kreis Gebote gab. –
Die drei beraubten mich; und der Halbteufel

To take my life. Two of these fellows you
Must know and own, this thing of darkness I
Acknowledge mine.

CALIBAN. I shall be pinch'd to death.
ALONSO. Is not this Stephano, my drunken butler?
SEBASTIAN. He is drunk now. Where had he wine?
ALONSO. And Trinculo is reeling ripe. Where should they
    Find this grand liquor that hath gilded 'em?
    How cam'st thou in this pickle?
TRINCULO. I have been in such a pickle since I saw you last that I fear me
    will never out of my bones. I shall not fear fly-blowing.

SEBASTIAN. Why, how now, Stephano?
STEPHANO. O, touch me not, I am not Stephano, but a cramp.

PROSPERO. You'ld be king o' the isle, sirrah?
STEPHANO. I should have been a sore one then.
ALONSO. This is a strange thing as e'er I look'd on.

Pointing to Caliban.

PROSPERO. He is as disproportion'd in his manners
    As in his shape. Go, sirrah, to my cell;
    Take with you your companions. As you look
    To have my pardon, trim it handsomely.
CALIBAN. Ay, that I will; and I'll be wise hereafter,
    And seek for grace. What a thrice-double ass
    Was I to take this drunkard for a god,
    And worship this dull fool!
PROSPERO. Go to, away!
ALONSO. Hence, and bestow your luggage where you found it.
SEBASTIAN. Or stole it, rather.

Exeunt Caliban, Stephano, and Trinculo.

PROSPERO. Sir, I invite your Highness and your train
    To my poor cell, where you shall take your rest
    For this one night; which, part of it, I'll waste
    With such discourse as, I not doubt, shall make it
    Go quick away – the story of my life,
    And the particular accidents gone by
    Since I came to this isle. And in the morn
    I'll bring you to your ship, and so to Naples,
    Where I have hope to see the nuptial
    Of these our dear-belov'd solemnized,

(Denn so ein Bastard ist er) war mit ihnen
Verschworen, mich zu morden. Ihr müsst zwei
Von diesen Kerlen kennen als die euren;
Und dies Geschöpf der Finsternis erkenn‘ ich
Für meines an.
CALIBAN. Ich werde tot gezwickt!
ALONSO. Ist dies nicht Stephano, mein trunkner Kellner?
SEBASTIAN. Er ist jetzt betrunken: wo hat er Wein gekriegt?
ALONSO. Und Trinculo ist auch zum Torkeln voll:
Wo fanden sie nur diesen Wundertrank,
Der sie verklärt? Wie kamst du in die Brühe?
TRINCULO. Ich bin so eingepökelt worden, seit ich Euch zuletzt sah, dass
ich fürchte, es wird nie wieder aus meinen Knochen herausgehn. Vor den
Schmeißfliegen werde ich sicher sein.
SEBASTIAN. Nun, Stephano, wie geht‘s?
STEPHANO. O rührt mich nicht an! Ich bin nicht Stephano, sondern ein
Krampf.
PROSPERO. Ihr wolltet hier auf der Insel König sein, Schurke?
STEPHANO. Da wär‘ ich ein geschlagner König gewesen.
ALONSO. Nie sah ich ein so seltsam Ding als dies.

Zeigt auf Caliban.

PROSPERO. Er ist so ungeschlacht in seinen Sitten
Als von Gestalt. – Geh, Schurk‘, in meine Zelle,
Nimm deine Spießgesellen mit: wo du
Vergebung wünschest, putze nett sie auf!
CALIBAN. Das will ich, ja; will künftig klüger sein
Und Gnade suchen: welch dreifacher Esel
War ich, den Säufer für 'nen Gott zu halten
Und anzubeten diesen dummen Narr‘n!
PROSPERO. Mach‘ zu! Hinweg!
ALONSO. Fort! Legt den Trödel ab, wo ihr ihn fandet!
SEBASTIAN. Vielmehr, wo sie ihn stahlen.

Caliban, Stephano und Trinculo ab.

PROSPERO. Ich lade Eure Hoheit nebst Gefolge
In meine arme Zell‘, um da zu ruhn
Für diese eine Nacht, die ich zum Teil
Mit solchen Reden hinzubringen denke,
Worunter sie, wie ich nicht zweifle, schnell
Wird hingehn: die Geschichte meines Lebens
Und die besondern Fälle, so geschehn,
Seit ich hierher kam; und am Morgen früh
Führ‘ ich euch hin zum Schiff und so nach Napel.
Dort hab‘ ich Hoffnung, die Vermählungsfeier
Von diesen Herzgeliebten anzusehn.

And thence retire me to my Milan, where
Every third thought shall be my grave.

ALONSO. I long
  To hear the story of your life, which must
  Take the ear strangely.
PROSPERO. I'll deliver all,
  And promise you calm seas, auspicious gales,
  And sail so expeditious, that shall catch
  Your royal fleet far off.

Aside to Ariel.

  My Ariel, chick,
  That is thy charge. Then to the elements
  Be free, and fare thou well! – Please you draw near. *Exeunt omnes.*

Epilogue

Spoken by Prospero.

  Now my charms are all o'erthrown,
  And what strength I have's mine own,
  Which is most faint. Now 'tis true,
  I must be here confin'd by you,
  Or sent to Naples. Let me not,
  Since I have my dukedom got,
  And pardon'd the deceiver, dwell
  In this bare island by your spell,
  But release me from my bands
  With the help of your good hands.
  Gentle breath of yours my sails
  Must fill, or else my project fails,
  Which was to please. Now I want
  Spirits to enforce, art to enchant,
  And my ending is despair,
  Unless I be reliev'd by prayer,
  Which pierces so, that it assaults
  Mercy itself, and frees all faults.
  As you from crimes would pardon'd be,
  Let your indulgence set me free. *Exit.*

Dann zieh‘ ich in mein Mailand, wo mein dritter
  Gedanke soll das Grab sein.
ALONSO. Mich verlangt
  Zu hören die Geschichte Eures Lebens,
  Die wunderbar das Ohr bestricken muss.
PROSPERO. Ich will es alles kund tun, und verspreche
  Euch stille See, gewognen Wind, und Segel
  So rasch, dass Ihr die königliche Flotte
  Weit weg erreichen sollt. –

Beiseite zu Ariel.

  Mein Herzens-Ariel,
  Dies liegt dir ob; dann in die Elemente!
  Sei frei und leb du wohl! – Beliebt‘s Euch, kommt! *Alle ab.*

Epilog

Von Prospero gesprochen.

Hin sind meine Zauberei‘n,
Was von Kraft mir bleibt, ist mein,
Und das ist wenig: nun ist‘s wahr,
Ich muss hier bleiben immerdar,
Wenn ihr mich nicht nach Napel schickt.
Da ich mein Herzogtum entrückt
Aus des Betrügers Hand, dem ich
Verziehen, so verdammet mich
Nicht durch einen harten Spruch
Zu dieses öden Eilands Fluch.
Macht mich aus des Bannes Schoß
Durch eure will‘gen Hände los.
Füllt milder Hauch aus Euerm Mund
Mein Segel nicht, so geht zu Grund
Mein Plan; er ging auf eure Gunst.
Zum Zaubern fehlt mir jetzt die Kunst;
Kein Geist, der mein Gebot erkennt;
Verzweiflung ist mein Lebensend‘,
Wenn nicht Gebet mir Hilfe bringt,
Welches so zum Himmel dringt,
Dass es Gewalt der Gnade tut
Und macht jedweden Fehltritt gut.
Wo ihr begnadigt wünscht zu sein,
Lasst eure Nachsicht mich befrein. *Ab.*

Content / Inhalt